NORTH CHESHIRE

Edited by Chris Hallam

First published in Great Britain in 2003 by
YOUNG WRITERS
Remus House,
Coltsfoot Drive,
Peterborough, PE2 9JX
Telephone (01733) 890066

All Rights Reserved

Copyright Contributors 2003

HB ISBN 1 84460 072 6
SB ISBN 1 84460 073 4

FOREWORD

Young Writers was established in 1991 as a foundation for promoting the reading and writing of poetry amongst children and young adults. Today it continues this quest and proceeds to nurture and guide the writing talents of today's youth.

From this year's competition Young Writers is proud to present a showcase of the best poetic talent from across the UK. Each hand-picked poem has been carefully chosen from over 66,000 'Hullabaloo!' entries to be published in this, our eleventh primary school series.

This year in particular we have been wholeheartedly impressed with the quality of entries received. The thought, effort, imagination and hard work put into each poem impressed us all and once again the task of editing was a difficult but enjoyable experience.

We hope you are as pleased as we are with the final selection and that you and your family will continue to be entertained with *Hullabaloo! North Cheshire* for many years to come.

Contents

Bollington Cross CE Primary School
Daniel Taylor	1
Angus Naylor	1
Annabel Crosby	2
Emma Connelly	2
David Brown	3
Nicholas Chadwick	3
Hayden Cooke	4
Tessa Blencathra Neale	4
Sara-Louise Bowring	5
Richard Millar	6
Ian Swindells	6
Danielle Faye Long	7
Ella Hilton	8
Christopher Tildsley	8
Daniel Bates	9
Megan Skelhorn	10
Elliott Simpson	11

Charles Darwin Primary School
Niall Flaherty	12
Megan Lloyd	12
Oliver Higgins	13
Bethany Lowe	14
Joshua Thompson	14
Hannah Woods	15
Krystel Gibson	16
Georgia May Miller	16
Ben Webber	17
Anne Marie Shields	17
Robyn Wells	18
Jacob Herbert	18

Crowton Christ Church CE Primary School
Melissa Penney	19
Bethany Sproston	20

Rachel Spanton	20
Thomas Holmes	21
Hannah Howman	22
Matthew Harley	22
Joshua Hodgkinson	23
Thomas Eaton	24
Jamie Owen	24
Ben Moores	25
Jessica Watson	25
Ben Clark	26
Jonathan McKeown	27
James Schofield	28
Jack Elson	28
Rachel Tunnacliffe	29

Dane Bank Primary School

Alex Penney	29
David Montgomery	30
Ben Melville	30
Jack McLellan	30
Joshua Crooks	31
Steven Quinn	31
Leonnie Bradshaw	32
Katie Pomfret	32
Rhea Ball	32
Ashleigh Worthington	33
Jessica Large	34
Luke Pirie	34
Jamie Hardman	35
Laura O'Toole	35
Joseph Costin	36
Natasha Reilly	36
Sascha Bradshaw	37
Sean Carey	37
Matthew Lindley	38
Jomo Pereira	38
Thomas Walker	39
Alysha Reilly	39

Laura Marshall	40
Jordan Whalley	40
Aimee Jenner	41
Daniel Street	41
Hannah O'Toole	42
Joseph Nuttall	42
Rebecca Maddocks	43
Nicole Amy Gibson	43
Charlotte Downs	44
Amy Regan	44
Daniel Matthews	45

Didsbury Road Primary School

Atoosa Mehralian	45
Jake Leonard	46
Katie Chisnall	46
Vogue Lucas	47
Alex Fenton	48
Peter Brown	48
Kerri-Leanne Taylor	49
Amy Clegg	50
Elizabeth Smith	50
Louise Ellis	51
Jonathan Edge	52
Jessica Sharp	52
Jack Cargill	53
Alexandra Watson	54
Jaydon Jones	54
Bethany Leonard	55
Darriel Booth	56
Rebecka Dalton	56
Chris Hand	57
Thomas Slevin	58
Amy Gill	58
Lauren McCullough	59
Becky Parker	60
Steven Galloway	61
Rachel Young	62

Lauren Thorpe	63
Liam Whelan	64
Alex Bolland	64
Joshua Harrison	65
Rachel Lennie	65
Felicia Farrimond	66
Chloe Lowry	66
Molly Temperley-Cassin	67
Ben Jolley	67
Nicola Brennan	68
Matthew Hartley	68
Asadullah Haider	69
Leon King	69
Tammy Aldawery	70
David Hayes	70
Yasmin Cooper	71
Pepy Wilson	71

Forest Park School

Aidan Morris	72
Matthew Vernon	72
Sean Savage	73
Amy McGuire	74
Callum Tipper	74
Natalie Graham	75
Christopher Duncan	76
Alex Warden	76
Sonia Kaur Bamrah	77
Nikhil Parmar	78
Nathan Lindo	78
Henry Mills	79
Elliott Davis	79
Katie Skinkis	80
Lauren Pye	80
Rachel Robinson	81
Jack McGuire	81
Jessica Foley	82

Golborne CP School
- Katie Johnson — 83
- Amy Lally — 84
- Emily Prior — 85
- Anthony Heesom — 86
- Craig Dale — 86
- Shauna Woodward — 87

Great Moor Junior School
- Joanna Steele — 88
- Faye Drinkwater — 88
- Joe Garnett — 89
- Jodhi Taylor — 90
- Heather Waterhouse — 90
- Bradley Webb — 91
- Jonathan Bramwell — 92
- Daniel Banfield — 92
- Alex Hopkins — 93
- Ellie Gaffney — 93
- Aaron Upton — 94
- Benjamin Johnson — 94
- Claire Carr — 95
- Ruby McLean — 95
- Helen Giles — 96
- Freddie McCoy — 96
- Joe Graham — 97
- Matthew Cookson — 97
- Michael Booth — 98

Holy Family RC Primary School
- Frances Reilly — 98
- Rebecca O'Brien — 99
- Laura Gardener — 99
- Michael Ranson — 100
- Saul Cooper — 100
- Laurence Francis — 101
- Lauren O'Brien — 101

Penketh South Primary School
Megan Comerford	102
Katherine Stephenson	102
Lauren Hoey	102
April Norton	103
Laura Cupit	103
Lucy Harrison	104
Calum Anderson	104
Kyle Jones	105
Andrew Smith	105
Martyn Driver	106
Steven Whitfield	106
Sarah Gore	106
Fara Raza	107
Joseph Brown	107
Kayleigh Kennedy	108
Sadie Kellett	108
Hayley Croft	109
Kara-Louise Royle	109
Charlotte Chadwick	110
Emily Sutton	110
Rebecca Green	111
Adam Mee	111
Rachael Scott	112
Bethany Bancroft	112
Rebecca Keoghan	113
Jack Giblin	113
Rebekah Caddick	114
Sarah Turner	114
Gary Loughead	115
Sophie Gilbertson	115
Nicola Warburton	115
Daniel McCarthy	116

St Basil's Catholic Primary School, Widnes
Jamie Sanderson	116
Natasha Tunstall	117
Paul Smith	117

Liam Codd	118
Chris McGowan	118
Leah Barton	118
Emily Rowlands	119
Chris Buckley	119
Suzanna Hughes	120
Lucy-May Amos Roscoe	121

St John the Evangelist CE Aided Primary School, Macclesfield

Daniel Seager	122
Jessica Taylor	122
Jodie Burgess	123
Matthew Taylor	124
Jack Rawlins	124
Jennifer Bucknell	125
Corinne Pinder	126
Imogen Ault	126
Emma Stell	127
Elizabeth Moss	128
Sophie Frith	128
Andrew Pickles	129
Charlotte Hyde	130
Sarah Sharpley	130
Cody Ives-Keeler	131
Naomi Thomas	132
Simone Longden	132
Rosie Barker	133
Abbey Dowse	134
Ashleigh Hehir	135
Gemma Brown	136
Elanah Grace Foster	137
Victoria Hordern	138
Oliver Gould	139
Leanne Melling	140
Rachel Ann Knight	141
Danielle L Hallworth	142
Jordan Riley	142
Stuart G Whittaker	143

Stefan Carney	143
Calum Robertson	144
Sam Lowe	144
Chloe Furness	145
Chris Holland	145
Sophie Avery	146
Joshua Thomas	146
Claire Taylor	147
Melanie Knight	147
Jordan Kenyon	148
Leah Gleaves	148
Eleanor Thomason	149
Robert Phythian	149
Alistair Williamson	150
James Moss	150
Abigail Walker	151
Rachel Barber	151
Hannah Davis	152
Duncan Littlechild	152
Charlotte Hobbs	153
Laura Baggs	153
Joel Frost	154
Eloise Cantwell	154
Jack Johnson	155
Ian Prior	155
Christopher Littlechild	156
Bethany Holt	156
Katie Bucknell	157
Sam Edwards	157
Nicola Pheasey	158
Jordan Bettany	158
Hannah Errington	159
Georgina Whitworth	159
Elisha Bradley	160
Chris Graves	160
Sam Avery	161

St Mary's CE Primary School, Sale
    Gabriel Derbyshire 161
    Laura Anderson 162
    Alexander Law 162
    Alexandra Cambridge 163

The Dale Primary School
    Sarah Potter 164
    Chris Barker 164
    Beth Hammett 165
    Callum Rogan 165
    Paul Harrison 166
    Holly Sunderland 166
    Matthew Jones 166
    Laura Bennett 167
    Matthew Griffiths 167
    Claire Faram 168
    Sarah Bowler 168
    Isabelle Willacy 169
    Rebecca Everett 170
    Mark Robinson 171
    Warren Parr 172
    Matthew Woolfenden 172

Weaverham Forest Primary School
    Joshua Adamson 173
    Abigail Edwards & Carolyn Tilston 173
    Jordan Furness 173
    Emily Mitchell 174
    Hannah Louise Rigby 174
    Sarah Baron 175
    Sarah Morris 175
    Siân White & Charlotte Dunne 176

The Poems

A NEW WORLD

A vast, deadly waterfall lies ahead,
Pounding down to deadly,
Razor-sharp rocks below.
Although he is scared and nervous,
He shows no fear.
The aliens are blood-thirsty, mud-dwelling monsters.
Alas, he thought, the end has come.
He falls down, down, down . . .
The aliens go down to feast.
They eat like frogs but are beasts.
The alien crafts are about to fly.
He sees one nearby.
He gets in and finds tin walls, very tall
And controls like balls.
He heard a low voice, terrified.
'Take me to Earth!'
'Okay,' he replied.

Daniel Taylor (8)
Bollington Cross CE Primary School

POEM

The Dean twisted down into the reservoir, like a sardine
Swimming violently. Beasts ran wildly through the vast
Undergrowth, hunting for their evening feasts. Cats
Ran round trees pawing at them trying to catch birds.
A rabbit dug a burrow in the ground at the foot of an old
Oak tree, the trees swayed slowly in the breeze. Harvest mice
Nibbled the corn in the fields, the frogs jumped into the
Reservoir. As the fox cubs played in the valley, the Dean
Twisted down into the reservoir, like a sardine swimming violently.

Angus Naylor (9)
Bollington Cross CE Primary School

POETRY

I gaze faintly into the moon –
It's like a vast pearl shimmering in the sunlight.
I see a spider crawling soundless,
Eyes dazzling vivid.
The pavement curve glistening,
While being viciously stood on.
A comet flew past briskly
And bashed barbarically
Into the moon . . .
I wish and wonder and that is all
Of the dreamless glisten of the moon.

Annabel Crosby (9)
Bollington Cross CE Primary School

MARS

Red is the colour of Mars,
Like strawberry jam in jars.
Lots and lots of stone,
You feel like you're at home.
Mars is very hot,
You can see lava a lot.
If you want to see stars,
Then land on Mars.
There's lots of trees,
So your dog might catch fleas.

Emma Connelly (9)
Bollington Cross CE Primary School

ANGRY PLANET

Jupiter, the angry planet:
Yellow, red, orange and white.
Comets and asteroids shooting by
At the speed of light.
A stormy planet
Covered in gas,
Flowing around the universe,
Orbiting the sun.
Jupiter, the angry planet:
Yellow, red, orange and white.

David Brown (9)
Bollington Cross CE Primary School

JUPITER

Jupiter, the gas giant,
Planet where no one lives.
The second brightest planet
Shining up above.
Colours that make an
Angry face
Far away in space.
A ring of dusty rocks
Spinning around with it.
Jupiter, the gas giant.

Nicholas Chadwick (9)
Bollington Cross CE Primary School

FIRE IN THE SKY

I found a land far from man,
The frigid rivers meandered and quickly ran,
At the posterior of a flailing tree,
Began a murky sunless sea,
Below its level, a creature breathing,
On a plankton-like substance it was feeding,
A fish rose past my peaceful planet,
Flashing lights blinded my fearless eyes.
The fish-like creature continued to rise -
Against a planet it will demise -
This hard ball of fire,
As tall as a spire,
My eyes deceived me,
I could not see,
What I desired to see,
Not a fish but a train of demolition,
Because this was my mission,
This journey for survival,
Which I am capable of,
I ran to my probe,
Then peered at my globe,
My engines began to rumble,
Then from my planet I started to tumble,
This sphere of frozen water,
I quickly raced past . . .

Hayden Cooke (9)
Bollington Cross CE Primary School

MY PLANET

Dark but cold with shimmering sand
I see two glistening, glowing eyes
They guide me to a sparkly land
I see silver glitter that looks like sand

I go on a walk through the shiny snow
I don't know why I'm walking so slow
There are birds in the sky that shimmer when you look
While you watch, you skate like a duck.

Tessa Blencathra Neale (9)
Bollington Cross CE Primary School

SUN SEED

I place my foot on the silver earth of ice.
I thought I was all alone.
I moved my face to see a woman,
With a flowing dress she was glowing,
Leaving a trail like a snail.
It started to rain -
Raining pearls.
I pick one - so I thought -
I dropped it -
A waterfall, I thought.
I walked through thinking something
Good will happen . . .
I see a boy
Holding a ball with spots, dead.
I planted a seed . . .
Gave him a feed . . .
The seed flew into the sky.
I thought, 'Well done.'
I gave them a sun.
They can have fun under the sun,
But it is still cold.
I say farewell.
A lady came up and said, 'Thank you.'
My name is Mell.

Sara-Louise Bowring (9)
Bollington Cross CE Primary School

A NEW WORLD

A vast, deadly waterfall lies ahead,
Pounding down to deadly
Razor-sharp rocks below.
Although he is scared and nervous,
He shows no fear.
The aliens are bloodthirsty, mud-dwelling monsters.
Alas, he thought, the end has come.
He falls down, down, down . . .
The aliens go down to feast.
They eat like frogs but are beasts.
The alien crafts are about to fly.
He sees one nearby.
He gets in and finds tin walls, very tall
And controls like balls.
He heard a low voice, terrified.
'Take me to Earth!'
'Okay,' he replied.

Richard Millar (9)
Bollington Cross CE Primary School

BLACK HOLE - SELL MY SOUL

I landed in a black hole,
I was about to sell my soul.
Just when I fell into another world,
I saw a giant whirl fading away.
The planet was a red, giant rock,
Too bad it did not have a clock.
I saw a cave when running from a wave.

They had a horrible sting,
Then a big thunderbolt hit the edge.
I jumped outside, I thought I was saved
But lava ran after me,
It was hot, I needed a fan,
It was cooler because of the wings of the flying thing.

Ian Swindells (9)
Bollington Cross CE Primary School

PLANET X!

I step on this planet,
Wondering why it is cold
And if it would behold,
A secret which is bold.
It had great frozen water cliffs,
That stood like big glass mountains
And lots of frozen waterfalls,
That glisten in the moonlight.
Suddenly everywhere turned black,
Not a sound to be heard.
Something touches my back,
I turn around and see a big bird!
For its head was as big as a football
And feet all sticky and webbed.
It looked at me like the *Devil!*
And as if to say, 'Get off my planet!'
So I ran with great heavy feet,
Back to my space shuttle,
Never to go there again.

Danielle Faye Long (9)
Bollington Cross CE Primary School

THE MARS MONSTER

A monster, a cold Mars monster,
Cracking the surface of Mars slowly,
It spent all its life inside hollow Mars.
Struggling to get to the top,
Making groaning noises, 'Referrer,'
As it's climbing up invisible steps.
This monster big and blue with a bright-red rim
And big starry eyes, it's name was Starry-Eye Surprise,
His giant blue body like rock,
Swaying from side to side, someone has just kicked him out
Of the centre of Mars.
Tears dripping down his lumpy face,
Green tears, very unusual creature.
I really want to know is there anymore of these marvellous creatures
Walking at 1 mile per hour?
It's trying to communicate with me, 'Eeeeerrrr.'
This creature has no friends, is lonely and looks
Positively ill!

Ella Hilton (9)
Bollington Cross CE Primary School

MY PLANETS

Jupiter is stormy
Jupiter looks angry
Jupiter is boiling
But Jupiter is king

Saturn has colourful rings
Saturn is beautiful
Saturn spins very fast
Causing ferocious winds

Comets are fast
Comets are dangerous
Comets are colourful
But comets are like a dirty snowball.

Christopher Tildsley (9)
Bollington Cross CE Primary School

ICE SAND

The icy desert with grains of icy sand.
There is not a sound on the beautiful ground.
A stream is running; icy pebbles cunning.
The glimmering ice is really nice.
Under the shining blue water,
I found a mound of ice,
With little creatures that looked like mice.
Talking creatures came down
And told me to go
Or they would make it snow!
I slid across the ice
When the ice lord came down.
He said, 'Leave this planet at once!'
I slipped into the freezing cold, shimmering water.
It made me invisible.
I started to worry,
I was in a hurry
To get back down to Earth.
I went into my spaceship,
I saw a bit of my lip . . .
It was wonderful how I got into my ship.
My fingers started to shrink.

Daniel Bates (9)
Bollington Cross CE Primary School

HEAVEN

A light year ago,
I flew a great white stallion
Into space.
I galloped past stars
After trotting on Mars,
Then I glided to galaxy five.
I landed on a planet
At 30 degrees,
The sun was fully blazed.
As I gazed through a wonderful stretch of land,
I heard a sound
Of trickling water.
My throat was parched,
As I started to find the tingling sound.
Streams like silver
And rivers of gold,
Glisten around this place
And sparkle on my face.
Rain like pears,
Hurl down from the sky.
'Ombraiotina,' came a chant
From behind.
I turned to find
An armoured wolf,
As big as a human,
Like a furry man.
'Oh dear, oh my,
What can I do?'
I cried.
He offered me an apple,
Like a ruby,
It was juicy,
I licked up.

Then he offered me a
Bronze cup
And in the cup was my soul,
I had died
And ridden a foal,
Up to paradise at the end of my life.

Megan Skelhorn (9)
Bollington Cross CE Primary School

I'VE BEEN TO A PLANET

I've been to a planet,
A very red planet,
With a temperature of -23°C.
I shouted, 'Yippee,' at -23°C.
I was right,
Now was the time to fly my kite.
I was a real pioneer.
Something hit my ear.
I turned, but nothing I found.
Then I saw a shadow on a rock behind,
A tickle went through my sock.
The shadow looked scared,
I dared
To see the one who had hit me.
I turned round to see,
There was nothing there . . .
I just stood and stared.
I cared about this day,
Wanting to see the one who cut my ear,
After all, I was a pioneer!

Elliott Simpson (9)
Bollington Cross CE Primary School

IT'S GOING DOWN

It's going down! Yes, the mobile's going
Abandoned, battered, old classroom
Is going down
Old, damp, unfriendly place
Is going down
Motionless, shattered, worn out
Is going down
But who?
By some men
No, they need machinery
A JCB!
Yes, that'll do the job
It's going down
Here it comes
The monstrous serial killer
Is taking it down
Horrible beast
Has taken it down!

Niall Flaherty (10)
Charles Darwin Primary School

GONE

Our old mobile
Standing there deserted
Monstrous beast rolling
Our thoughts locked inside
Only bad memories

Dangerous criminal ready to murder
Our helpless mobile getting battered
Wood splintering, glass shattering
Mobile getting crushed to pieces, until
Gone.

Megan Lloyd (9)
Charles Darwin Primary School

SCHOOL IS...

School is a dark, dull cloud, always ready to rain,
School is an old lady's shop, full of boring stuff,
School is a murderer's home, goat skulls lying about everywhere,
School is a fearsome torture pit, homing in on unsuspecting victims,
School is a long book with not one single colour or picture in,
School is an endless period of boredom, wearing away our pitiful minds,
School is a cunning vulture, circling its prey,
School is a strict army, packed full of rules,
School is library, as quiet as a mouse,
School is a jail, we come in chains and steel balls,
School is a noisy quarry, full of impossible work,
School is a bloody war between teachers and pupils,
School is a never-ending car chase of lunch money,
School is game of chess, you have no chance of winning,
School is a brainwashing machine, working its way into our tiny,
                                                  pea-size brains,
School is a dark, red hell.

Oliver Higgins (10)
Charles Darwin Primary School

GONE!

Our lonely, frail mobile crumbled like a soft biscuit,
Fragile panes of window crashed down like a waterfall of glass,
Slashing at the frail structure like a tamer hitting a defenceless lion,
Tearing,
Gnawing,
Snapping and crunching, the heartless beast
Destroyed a lifetime of secrets locked inside forever,
Dirty, thick, brown water oozed out of a dripping drain,
Violently landing on cold, brutal ground,
Abandoned waste trying to say sorry,
Too late!
Hungry monster devouring its scared, isolated prey,
Finished nibbling,
It was empty and deserted,
Going, going, going, gone,
A forgotten wooden pile remains.

Bethany Lowe (9)
Charles Darwin Primary School

SCHOOL IS . . .

School is a tall tree, with many branches and thousands of leaves.
School is a huge town centre, full of busy workers.
School is a patch of rabbit warrens, as rabbits appear here and there.
School is an educational library, as we learn some necessary facts.
School is a finger, only part of a one big body.
School is a box containing loads of busy ants.

School is a white prison cell, sometimes dull.
School is an open book, lying on a table for everyone to share.
School is a berry bush, full of ripe berries.
School is a meeting area, where friends and family come to gather.
School is a world full of brightness and wonder.
School is a painting, colourful and amazing.

Joshua Thompson (10)
Charles Darwin Primary School

DEAD

Standing lifeless
All alone
Nothing to be done
Nothing to be told
Monstrous beast tearing up our classroom

Helping not a choice
Crashing to the floor
Like cardboard being ripped apart
Bullying it to the floor
Once it stood
No more
Cruelly torn apart

Two classrooms were there
Not anymore
Been demolished to the floor
Came for another blow that JCB.

Hannah Woods (10)
Charles Darwin Primary School

THE TERMINATION

Our mobile stood there innocently,
Not a muscle to move, no legs to run on
When a monster pounces on its prey.
The beast devoured the delicious food in minutes,
Tearing viciously at skin and flesh.
Its young cub tramped over the skeletal remains.
Graffiti walls collapsed as the monster wounded the lifeless corpse,
She sped away to catch another bit of flesh for her young,
Just a river of wood and glass,
Happy life,
Terrible ending,
One memory forgotten,
Another remembered.

Krystel Gibson (10)
Charles Darwin Primary School

SCHOOL IS!

School is a flock of beautifully painted birds,
School is a busy beehive,
School is as cruel as Azkaban with 15 angry dementors,
School is a bunch of freshly-picked flowers,
School is a vase of magic water,
School is a bunch of golden grapes from magic vines forever
                                                          growing stronger,
School is a row of rainbow-coloured bottles, sitting on an
                                                           old brick wall,
School is a big box of chocolates waiting to be opened at 9:00,
School is a sea of dolphins forever swimming.

Georgia May Miller (10)
Charles Darwin Primary School

DESTROYED

Violent, ruthless, destructive, mean monster
Crashed his gigantic trunk
Smashing the delicate, powerless, wooden hut
Wet, damp mobile
It clawed at the dilapidated classroom

His gigantic teeth
Biting chunks of flimsy wood

The beast snared at torn fragments
Shattered windows

The broken room
Stood there
An unused piece of furniture
Fell.

Ben Webber (9)
Charles Darwin Primary School

THERE IT GOES

Climbing restlessly, stretching its clutched hand out.
As angry as a lion, the delicate mobile suddenly was devoured.
Watching as the brutal claw of an orc cold-bloodedly destroys its terrified prey.
Lying there in pain, killed by a cruel, crunching creature.
Smashed up, like a crumpled body.
Wickedly the creature jumps and growls, crunching his legs as he lands.

Anne Marie Shields (10)
Charles Darwin Primary School

GOING, GOING, GONE

Hungry monster viciously tearing apart our defenceless mobile,
Black water oozing out from the broken water pipe,
Slashing beast devouring its prey like a brutal lion,
Windows shattering like frozen ice on a freezing day,
Graffitied walls violently crashing to the ground,
A crumbling biscuit,
Battered building fell as sadly as the Twin Towers,
Delicate classrooms being torn down onto the brutal ground,
Our neglected old friend fell down like a waterfall of wood,
Dusty remains of our abandoned friend,
Our first room in year five,
Going,
    Going,
        Gone!

Robyn Wells (10)
Charles Darwin Primary School

SHATTERED, OLD MOBILE COLLAPSING TO THE GROUND

A rusty, staggering mobile,
Standing as still as a statue,
A jiggering, crunching beast,
Sprung into action like a monster catching his wounded prey,
Vulnerable, ancient mobile terrorised,
A brutal beast staring at him,
He moved his heartless mechanical arms,
Pulled the building down,
Falling,
    Falling,
        Smash!

Jacob Herbert (9)
Charles Darwin Primary School

STARS!

There it goes, a shooting star,
Away it goes, far, far, far,
Up in the sky,
Like a silver dragonfly.

The stars so bright,
Shine only at night,
Swirling and swooping,
But still they aren't drooping.

Millions of stars are always there,
In the white misty air,
In the pinky atmosphere,
Millions of stars are always near.

The stars have always been,
Where they can be seen,
The stars of the sky will never go,
That's a fact we all know!

No one's going to beat
The North Star shining at no one's defeat,
It's so bright tonight,
Brighter than any other night.

In one big galaxy,
There are lots of stars shining free,
Lots of glowing stars,
You can see them from Mars.

The sun is the biggest of them all,
All the others look so small,
All the planets orbit the sun,
It looks like good fun.

Melissa Penney (10)
Crowton Christ Church CE Primary School

THE COUNTRYSIDE

Miles and miles of greenery,
An ocean of land.
Magnificent, inviting scenery,
Encaptures us all around.

Rushing rivers swimming by,
Floating clouds in the sky.
Birds that glide within the air,
Animals wandering freely there.

Smells of lush grass,
Flowers within the paths.
Lambs around are leaping,
Whilst foxes lay sleeping.

Seasons change within this place,
The sense of peace remains
An everlasting tranquil base,
The countryside sustains.

Bethany Sproston (9)
Crowton Christ Church CE Primary School

THE TRIBAL HUNTSMAN

The rival men, the rival men
Are here to hunt me down,
Tracing in my footprints,
Here with their nasty frown.

The rival men, the rival men,
Clutching their spears and knives,
Running for days,
Ruining our lives.

The rival men, the rival men,
Ready to kill, ready to kill,
Exposing their weapons
And all was still.

The rival men, the rival men
Have hunted me down.
They've traced in my footprints
And left with their nasty frown.

Rachel Spanton (10)
Crowton Christ Church CE Primary School

I WISH I WAS A WOOLLY HAT

I wish I was a woolly hat,
To keep heads warm all day.
I wish I was a woolly hat,
From breakfast to midday.

I wish I was a woolly hat,
Perhaps a bobbly one.
I wish I was a woolly hat,
It would be such fun!

I wish I was a woolly hat,
Not a topper or a cap.
I wish I was a woolly hat,
A designer one from Gap!

I wish I was a woolly hat,
Or a pot of gold.
A woolly hat's not the life for me,
I'm not one for the cold!

Thomas Holmes (11)
Crowton Christ Church CE Primary School

MICHAEL'S 4TH BIRTHDAY

It was Michael's fourth birthday and a surprise was in store,
Mr Blobby was coming, we hadn't seen him before,
Sandwiches, cakes and lots of juice too,
Lots of nice things to eat, just for me and you.

Now for the party games, I hope that I will win,
A balloon or pencils, not wrappers to put in the bin,
Pass the parcel, musical chairs and statues too,
Must not move a muscle; it's very hard to do.

Knock, knock, knock, there's someone at the door,
Its Mr Blobby, children quick all sit on the floor,
Oh no it's not, it's a monster pounding in,
Running and jumping making a horrible din.

Mummy, Mummy, tell him to go away,
I am too scared for this to happen today,
It's OK kids, no need to worry,
It's only Michael's uncle Gary.

Hannah Howman (9)
Crowton Christ Church CE Primary School

MY PETS

My pets are the best,
Better than all the rest,
My guinea pig is as quick as lightning,
It can be quite frightening!

I feed them every day
And keep them warm with hay,
I clean them out each Sunday
And play with them after a school day.

I would like to take my rabbit on a lead,
But it would look quite funny,
To see a bunny on a lead,
Bouncing down the lane!

Matthew Harley (10)
Crowton Christ Church CE Primary School

THE FLYING BOX

Once I had a cardboard box,
It was strong and tall
And when I tried to pick it up
It just wouldn't budge at all.

I was only three you see,
So that's why I called,
I called my mum to help me,
But she just stopped and stalled.

So I decided what to do,
I tried painting it a very light-blue,
But I got quite carried away
And painted the carpet and my shoe!

I made my box into a plane
And took it outside but it started to rain,
I was going to have a test flight for one,
I left it outside and went in feeling glum.

To my amazement it started to fly,
Fly way up high into the sky,
I couldn't believe my eyes you see,
But always remember I was only three!

Joshua Hodgkinson (9)
Crowton Christ Church CE Primary School

A Day In The Life Of Phoebe, My Cat

Phoebe wakes up
Eats
Sleeps
Wakes up
Goes outside
Comes in
Eats
Sleeps
Wakes up
Gets stroked
And sleeps.

Thomas Eaton (9)
Crowton Christ Church CE Primary School

Nearly Spring

Snowdrops with bobbing
Heads so white.
Crocus bulbs
Pushing through the hard soil with
All their might.

Just to watch this wonderful
Thing.

Must mean that surely it is
Nearly spring!

Jamie Owen (8)
Crowton Christ Church CE Primary School

ONE TO TEN . . . AND BACK AGAIN

One silver paperclip in my little tin
Two smelly socks in the laundry bin
Three rubber ducks in my bubble bath
Four silly jokes that make me laugh
Five shiny marbles rolling on the floor
Six baseball caps hanging on my door
Seven noisy friends bouncing on my bed
Eight fat teddies, one with a big head
Nine big pictures hanging on my wall
Ten yummy sweets that are very small

Ten cuddly toys that sit on my shelf
Nine raisin cookies that I made myself
Eight popped footballs lying in the yard
Seven pages of maths which are very hard
Six fun books that I read every day
Five computer games that I love to play
Four sizzling sausages cooking for my tea
Three of my Frisbees stuck in a tree
Two stink bombs gassing out the room
One angry mum shooing me with her broom.

Ben Moores (9)
Crowton Christ Church CE Primary School

PENGUINS

I saw a penguin one day,
It wiggled a bit,
It jiggled a bit!
My sister wanted a cuddle,
But it cuddled *me* instead!

Jessica Watson (9)
Crowton Christ Church CE Primary School

AGGRESSIVE ANIMALS

Shark, shark - beware of the shark,
One day he might turn up in the park,
Shark, shark, watch that shark;
Because he might just eat Ben Clark.

Crocodile, crocodile - beware of the crocodile,
Don't ever trust his smile,
For that massive beasty,
May just eat you in a while.

Alligator, alligator - beware of him,
He's a slippery one, who'll get you when you swim,
So watch out for that alligator,
He may just eat you later!

Bear, bear - beware of that old bear,
If you meet him in the dark, you may get a scare,
So if you dare to see that bear,
Run, run, run - just like a hare.

Lion, lion - beware of that lion,
Watch out for his big teeth and hair,
Coz if he takes a bite out of you,
You'll always have a nightmare.

Aggressive animals, come in all shapes,
Large, fat, small, big and thin,
So look out for these assorted beasties,
In case they might just get in!

Ben Clark (9)
Crowton Christ Church CE Primary School

MY BASKET OF CARS

I have a basket that is quite big,
In my basket I have loads of cars.
One is like a spaceship,
It could be from Mars!

Some of them are from America,
My favourite is a Corvette Stingray.
I play with some of the cars sometimes,
But the Corvette I play with every day!

One day I got a load out,
I drove them into long queues.
I sorted them into colours,
Reds, yellows, greens and blues!

Some are army, some are planes,
Some go fast, some just crawl,
Some are large, some are small,
I don't care, I like them all!

I have a few car tracks,
One of them has a road that goes in a sort of circle.
It has a garage in the middle,
Its sign is blue and purple.

I've had my basket for as long as I can remember.
I play with my cars from January to December!
My basket has brought me so much joy,
I'm going to keep it for my own little boy!

Jonathan McKeown (10)
Crowton Christ Church CE Primary School

My Nan's Big Dog

My nan's big dog has
Grey and black spots.

My nan's big dog can
Jump fences about 1m tall.

My nan's dog is very
Soft, cute and cuddly.

But best of all
She's my nan's dog!

James Schofield (11)
Crowton Christ Church CE Primary School

A Walk Through The Forest

Birds singing, twittering out loud.
Snakes sliding along the grass,
Spiders crawling and killing all day.
The ants are busy, making nests
And busy bees making honey.
The worms sliding along, eating the soil
Creatures,
A peaceful place, full of life!

Jack Elson (10)
Crowton Christ Church CE Primary School

MY CAT

My cat sits twitching its tail
By the bowl of the goldfish,
Eyes glowing like flames,
Expecting to get its wish.

At other times she climbs the tree,
Running up like a flash,
Her ears prick up and listen,
Before she topples and falls with a crash.

In summer, she watches the birds
And patiently lies in wait,
And tries her best to pounce and kill,
But often leaves it too late.

But my favourite view of my cat
Is as she lies by the fire and purrs,
She's curled like a snail, all snug and tight,
No care of the world is hers.

Rachel Tunnacliffe (9)
Crowton Christ Church CE Primary School

HULLABALOO

A big yellow brass trumpet trumpeting in a brass band,
A giant dinosaur roaring in hunger,
A purple, red, blue and yellow firework exploding in the dark sky,
A girl screaming on a long red roller coaster,
A scary tiger chewing at his catch,
A rocket's engine making a deafening sound as it starts its
                              space adventure.

Alex Penney (10)
Dane Bank Primary School

HULLABALOO!

A spotted cheetah roaring for its family in the open fields,
A black cow mooing for its mum in grassy plains,
A Ferrari's engine roaring past the finish line,
A fire crackling in the blazing building,
The viper zooming in the entrance at Six Flags over Georgia,
A classroom full of noisy kids at Dane Bank,
A raptor in tall grass plains like a T-rex in the jungle roaring
Away other predators with its mighty battle roar,
What a great hullabaloo!

David Montgomery (11)
Dane Bank Primary School

A HULLABALOO

A shaggy dog barking on a sunny day,
A large monkey chattering whilst they were trying to play,
A small bird tweeting on a horrible night,
A little kitten miaowing but I thought it was trying to fight,
A tiny fluffy rabbit crunching on its food,
A massive lion roaring as well as it being rude,
A hairy horse neighing and running around,
A large-eyed owl hooting over a mouse it's found.

Ben Melville (11)
Dane Bank Primary School

WHAT A HULLABALOO

Boys playing football, shouting and yelling,
Cricket balls crashing into the wickets,
Rally cars speeding around the corners,
Little girls screaming on a scary ride,

Hockey players crashing into the barriers,
My grandad's asleep and he is snoring,
The doors slam in the palace,
Egg chasers slamming into the posts.

Jack McLellan (9)
Dane Bank Primary School

HULLABALOO!

A wild dog running through the grassy park,
Like a lion running through the forest's ferny floor,
A baby crying as if life were useless
And it was never going to end,
A lonely child on the PlayStation all day,
Completing game by game, with no care for anyone or anything,
A useless poem and a child writing, bore, bore, bore
And a teacher shouting, 'More, more, more!'
Oh, what a crazy hullabaloo!

Joshua Crooks (10)
Dane Bank Primary School

HULLABALOO

A Rottweiler barking at a crying baby,
Hailstones hitting a double-glazed window,
A car skidding to a halt at a red light,
Cats singing on a brick wall and a boot hitting them,
Ocean waves hitting the sea wall,
A fire burning anything in its path like
A lion looking for its prey,
A crowd cheering for David Beckham scoring a goal.

Steven Quinn (10)
Dane Bank Primary School

HULLABALOO

Loud children shouting in the classroom,
Crashing giant waves at the seaside,
Motorbikes starting, horrible and noisy,
Children dragging chairs along the floor,
My noisy dog barking a lot in the garden,
People screaming in the playground,
Someone messing with their pans,
My sister on the computer with the volume right up,
Teachers shouting at children in PE.

Leonnie Bradshaw (8)
Dane Bank Primary School

WHAT A HULLABALOO

I heard a moan,
I heard a groan,
You heard me yelling on the telephone.
The swings go creak,
The doors go *eek*
And now my sister's going to speak.
I won't drop the vase on the floor,
But Nanna says, 'Don't slam the door.'

Katie Pomfret (9)
Dane Bank Primary School

HULLABALOO

The beep of a car driving past,
The sound of children playing,
The sound of chalk screeching down a blackboard,
The sound of chattering children,
The screech of a chair,

The sound of people walking past,
The sound of owls hooting in trees,
The sound of tweeting birds,
The sound of people chatting in shops,
What a noisy hullabaloo.

Rhea Ball (10)
Dane Bank Primary School

WHAT A HULLABALOO

Someone's moaning,
Someone's groaning,
Someone called Ann
Smells of a thing in a pan.
Ring of a phone,
A dog eating a bone,
That noise is loud,
A picture in a cloud.
A drink is leaking,
People are speaking,
That road is long,
I like that song.
There is a door,
Look, people are poor,
This is a big city,
Oh, what a pity.
My sister's big,
I like to play tig,
I have long hair,
A breath of fresh air.
What a hullabaloo!

Ashleigh Worthington (9)
Dane Bank Primary School

HULLABALOO

My sister in her bedroom singing like she is crying,
The noise of my toy cupboard door when I close it,
The noise of my sister's bricks when she knocks them on the floor,
My sister when she wears her clonky boots on our wooden floor,
Dogs making a racket when they are barking,
The oven when my mum or dad turns it on,
My sister in the night when she cries if she has had a nightmare
                                                          and wakes me up,
The tingling noise of pennies,
The noise of the kettle getting ready to make a cup of tea,
The smashing plates on the floor when I do the washing up.
What a horrible hullabaloo!

Jessica Large (7)
Dane Bank Primary School

HULLABALOO!

A big elephant blowing its nose,
An enormous hot air balloon being popped by a bird's beak in the countryside,
Doors slamming loudly in my house,
A firework going off in the back garden,
A rocket flying up to the moon,
A plane taking off at Manchester airport,
My teacher shouting in the classroom,
A lion roaring loudly in the dark basement,
An exhaust on a racing car,
A helicopter taking off.

Luke Pirie (7)
Dane Bank Primary School

HULLABALOO

A police siren when there is a nasty emergency,
Some very loud fireworks going off last night,
When construction is going on when a house has been knocked down,
When the loud storm was raging a week ago,
When Mr Cruden is shouting when he is in a temper,
When people shout down my ear,
When people slam doors in school,
When Miss Bishop shouts at us,
When motorbikes start their engines,
When my heater goes off and on at home,
What a hullabaloo.

Jamie Hardman (8)
Dane Bank Primary School

HULLABALOO!

A fast ride at Alton Towers crashing against the sides of the track,
A big brown dog crying outside in the rain,
A mean teacher shouting at a boy daydreaming,
A girl going mad at her mum for grounding her,
A drunk man stumbling into tables in the pub,
A cow mooing in the grassy fields,
A piano playing by itself – spooky!
A car going side to side on the ice (cracking),
A mouse nibbling on a piece of cheese.

Laura O'Toole (10)
Dane Bank Primary School

HULLABALOO!

A wailing of a baby crying for its rattle,
Little kids in the park saying, *'Wee!'* as they go down the slide,
My sister shouting, 'Can I play?' down my ear,
The roaring of a lion hunting for food,
Recorders screeching with holes not covered properly,
Mums on the phone talking about junk,
The crying of kids getting told off,
Girls talking about gel pens,
Cars screeching down the road,
The laughing of kids in a snowball fight,
What an irritating hullabaloo!

Joseph Costin (9)
Dane Bank Primary School

HULLABALOO!

An old bike screeching down the narrow street,
A teacher scratching her nails down the small blackboard,
A pack of lions roaring in the busy zoo because they are hungry,
A group of children shouting in the grassy park,
A lifeguard echoing to the naughty children in the lively
                                        swimming pool,
A swarm of bees buzzing as they fly through the sunny garden,
Children laughing at the bad joke someone has just told,
A dog barking as he runs down the street to his house,
What a terrible hullabaloo.

Natasha Reilly (10)
Dane Bank Primary School

A HORRIBLE HULLABALOO!

Children yelling loudly down the narrow street,
As they stamp their big feet;
Shaggy dogs scratching at the dark door,
All you can hear is stamping on the floor;
Dogs barking as loud as they can,
People telling them off like a man;
All you can hear is shouting,
As their mum gives them a clouting,
But what a terrible noise,
It's made by all the boys.

Sascha Bradshaw (10)
Dane Bank Primary School

HULLABALOO

The booming of fireworks on a dark night,
Babies screaming for their mums,
Guns fired with a bang for no good reason,
People crying for their lives in terror,
A sinking ship with a splash,
A workman drilling through the floor,
Everyone shouting at the same time,
The animals of the world talking, talking,
Bombs flying through the air like seagulls,
Now that's what I call a *hullabaloo!*

Sean Carey (10)
Dane Bank Primary School

HULLABALOO

The great roller coaster rushes by loudly,
Children scream and squeal as a mouse scuttles across the floor,
Football fans cheer as a player scores a great goal,
Motorbikes rev noisily at the start of a race,
Bombs explode very loudly during the dreadful World War II,
A vacuum cleaner roars as cleaners vac the school carpet,
Glass crashes as a kid kicks a football through a window by accident,
A huge firework exploding in the sky on Bonfire Night,
Car brakes screeching on a road. Too late!
Kids cheer as the school holidays begin, hooray!
What a horrendous hullabaloo!

Matthew Lindley (11)
Dane Bank Primary School

HULLABALOO

People screaming loudly in their big drive,
Big cars crashing on the noisy roads,
Builders dropping hard bricks,
My mum when she is mad at me,
My sister crying in my house because she got a hard slap off my dad,
Me, when I have fallen off my bike outside,
People slamming doors at home,
Cars driving on the road,
The teachers shouting loud in school,
People ringing the bell in my house.

Jomo Pereira (7)
Dane Bank Primary School

WHAT A HULLABALOO!

Doors creaking in a spooky castle,
Brothers yelling in the living room,
Sisters crying as loud as can be,
Dads shouting very loud,
Noisy thunder all over the place,
Beyblades banging as loud as they can,
Bulls stomping as loud as the thunder,
Eagles screeching making a big racket,
Ringing telephones making a big din,
Ducks quacking, yelling, screaming and shouting,
Mirrors smashing making big clatters,
What a hullabaloo!

Thomas Walker (8)
Dane Bank Primary School

WHAT A TERRIBLE HULLABALOO!

My class is loud,
You can hear them up in the cloud,
Sometimes I wish,
They were more quiet than this!
Some people are moaning,
Others are groaning.
They knock off the roof,
But they don't shout out the truth,
I wish I could shut them up,
Tut, tut, tut!
What a terrible hullabaloo!

Alysha Reilly (9)
Dane Bank Primary School

HULLABALOO

The screeching of a blackboard
While I am trying to work,
Rustling leaves in the woods
Really freaks me out,
The chattering of people
Gets on my nerves,
The banging of a truck next to my house
Whilst I am doing my homework,
The mooing of a cow
That has escaped from a field,
My parents showing off in the streets
Really embarrasses me,
Cats miaowing at birds
While I am playing out,
What a horrible hullabaloo.

Laura Marshall (9)
Dane Bank Primary School

HULLABALOO!

Clanging of a roller coaster making me dizzy,
Revving of a motorbike trying to wake me up,
Screeching of a blackboard while I am trying to work,
Chattering of my mum when I want to go,
Loud rumbling of my belly when I am hungry,
Shaking of my top bunk when there is a rumble,
Howling of an owl in the trees,
Mooing of a cow while it's having milk taken,
Snorting of pigs on the farm,
Matthew screeching while I'm on the phone.

Jordan Whalley (10)
Dane Bank Primary School

HULLABALOO

Children in the class, shouting loud,
The school bell ringing that's really noisy,
My brother shouting and yelling because he's cross with me,
Miss Bishop shouting at the top of her voice,
Large tigers roaring in the dark jungle,
Doors slamming whilst I'm in bed,
The telly on as loud as it will get,
My brother shouting, 'It's really wet,'
Children shouting in the playground,
My puppy barking in the middle of the night,
What a hullabaloo!

Aimee Jenner (8)
Dane Bank Primary School

WHAT A HULLABALOO

Footballs smashing into nets
When Dad is sleeping in the chair,
Golf balls sweeping into holes,
Hockey players crashing into corners,
Basketballs banging up and down,
Rugby balls flying over the line,
Wrestlers crashing out of the ring,
Boxers getting knocked out,
Skateboarders skidding round and round,
What a hullabaloo.

Daniel Street (8)
Dane Bank Primary School

HULLABALOO

Skipping ropes hitting the floor,
Hula-hoops rolling round the playground,
Boys playing football, yelling and shouting,
Children running round,
Alarm clocks ringing,
Little dogs barking,
Church bells ringing,
Old men snoring,
Babies screaming for a bottle,
Adults chatting in the park,
All the teachers laughing
And there was such a hullabaloo!

Hannah O'Toole (9)
Dane Bank Primary School

HULLABALOO

Doors slamming loudly in school,
Children screaming in school,
People banging metal on my gate,
Children in my house,
The toilet flushing in my gran's house,
The teacher shouting loudly in the school,
Someone smashing glass in my house,
Someone throwing toys in my nan's house,
Rockets blasting off.

Joseph Nuttall (7)
Dane Bank Primary School

HULLABALOO

Children in the playground, screaming, shouting and yelling,
Enormous and noisy lions in the dark jungle,
Crying babies in their warm cots because they need a new nappy,
Fire engines coming to put out a giant fire,
Discos with the loudest music ever!
Tigers roaring in the deep, dark, scary jungle,
Fighting in the noisy war that we never want again,
Car engines zooming down the motorway,
Chairs scraping in the noisy classroom,
The school bell ringing when it's time to go back in, *boo hoo*,
What a noisy hullabaloo.

Rebecca Maddocks (8)
Dane Bank Primary School

HULLABALOO

The sound of a cow mooing in the field,
The loud sound of Class 5 chatting when we are working,
The loud sound of the blackboard screeching when I am working,
The very loud sound of a guitar when my brother is playing,
The sound of a hooting owl looking for its prey,
The sound of shouting in the playground when they are playing tig,
The sound of the bell that gives me earache,
The sound of Miss Megson shouting when we are too noisy,
The sound of the steel band when Mr Sinclair is trying to teach us,
The sound of a fire engine rushing to put a fire out,
What a noisy hullabaloo.

Nicole Amy Gibson (9)
Dane Bank Primary School

HULLABALOO

Noisy brothers in the bedroom,
Playing, shouting, bouncing on the bed,
Tigers roaring in the scary jungle,
Mum shouting in the bathroom,
Chairs scraping on the busy floor,
Dad's terrible singing in the shower,
Children in the classroom shouting loudly,
Loud, frightening thunder, scary lightning in the sky,
Miss Bishop shouting loud,
A school bell makes a loud noise, it makes me shiver,
Cars roaring past the school,
What a hullabaloo!

Charlotte Downs (8)
Dane Bank Primary School

HULLABALOO

Children in the classroom shouting loud,
Children in the classroom stamping their feet on the
                              squeaking floorboards,
Mum shouting, 'Go to bed.'
Children shouting in the playground,
Dog barking at the ginger cat,
People banging at the window,
People crying in the bathroom,
Big, old books falling on the floor,
Pens squeaking on the board,
Shutters closing at night.

Amy Regan (8)
Dane Bank Primary School

WHAT A HULLABALOO

When I get out of bed
and my mum's shouting, 'Ned!'

I go downstairs,
I get some pairs

Of socks out of the box,
I hear some knocks.

I go to school
and swim in the pool.

I wash the plates,
I meet my mates.

They go to the park,
they are there 'til it's dark.

Daniel Matthews (8)
Dane Bank Primary School

FIREWORKS

Zooming, sparkling, spinners,
Gangling, spangling, smoky dragons
Splashes of sparks flying in the sky
Sparklers lighting up your face
Crashing, booming rockets
Exploding boxes that you get shocked by
At the end, it woke everyone up.

Atoosa Mehralian (10)
Didsbury Road Primary School

BUT BACK TO SCHOOL

I vote, holidays rule
I also vote that school's drool

In the pool you pretend to sink
But back at school you have to think

You can play in the sun
But back at school it's just no fun

You can enjoy your tasty ice creams
But back at school frustration screams

You are laughing at your mates
But back at school your homework waits

I have to leave my brand new friend
But back at school my joy will end

I haven't done my homework now
But back at school will be my teacher's row.

Jake Leonard (10)
Didsbury Road Primary School

A DAY AT THE ZOO

I'm off to the zoo
With my mum
We're going to take a picnic
Yum, yum, yum

I'm off to see the lions
Won't it be nice
I do like the tigers
I might see them twice

The penguins are my favourite
They're always great
They look like waiters
Bringing my plate

It's dark in the bat cave
Some people scream
I think it's really funny
Now where's that ice cream?

Katie Chisnall (10)
Didsbury Road Primary School

PENGUIN POEM

I'm a penguin,
Short and fat,
I jump in icy water
And catch a sprat.

I'm a penguin,
Short and thin,
I waggle my wings,
Which look like fins.

I'm a penguin,
With cold feet,
I eat
Seal meat.

I'm a penguin,
That can't fly,
So now you know,
I don't lie.

Vogue Lucas (10)
Didsbury Road Primary School

THE CLEVER BULL

There once was a bull to who it was plain
To everyone else that he had a big brain
He worked out sums while lying in bed
There wasn't a book he had not read
But there was an answer he could not work out
What was life really all about?
He thought all night, he thought all day
He only found out one morning in May,
'I've got it, I've worked it out!'
You should have been there, (it wasn't half a shout!)
'They want my beef, they want my leather!
Oh dear, I better tell my best friend, Heather!'
The next day out came farmer Mound,
So clever bull pushed him to the ground
And all you kids, don't you worry,
Farmer Mound won't be back in a hurry
And to get his revenge for his threatened life,
He even ran off with the farmer's wife!

Alex Fenton (10)
Didsbury Road Primary School

THE PLACE

There is a place where you can go
You can roll and sledge on heavy snow
Know and hear all top-dog news
Run and jump and crawl and snooze

Whisper, shout and screech and laugh
There's no such thing as work or staff
School is gone, closed long ago
Not going back there, no, no, no

I am feeling pretty fine
Oh my god, look at the time
Mum says it's time to go
Why? I will never know.

Peter Brown (11)
Didsbury Road Primary School

THE TERROR

The terror lurks inside my house,
Is it a monster or is it a mouse?
It might be green, it might be blue,
There could be one or more than two!

It could have fangs or could have claws,
Or maybe, even, could have paws.
It could be big or could be small,
It may be short or even tall!

The terror could be round and fat,
Or even look like a baseball bat!
It might have eyes or might not,
Would it be cold or would it be hot?

The terror might have an amazing odour
Of mouldy cheese growing older and older.
It might smell like stinky socks,
Or even mould starting to rot!

But one thing is sure, I know,
I have to tell you before I go,
The little terror is my bruv,
Though he's bad, he's the one I love!

Kerri-Leanne Taylor (11)
Didsbury Road Primary School

Do This, Do That

Parents, do this, do that,
Tidy your room,
Feed that cat,
Do this, do that.
Make some tea,
Now clean that mat,
Do this, do that.
Don't eat crisps,
They'll make you fat,
Do this, do that.
Brush your teeth,
Wash that hat,
Do this, do that.
Don't sit down,
Get rid of that bat,
Do this, do that.
Phone Uncle George,
Phone Auntie Pat!
Why should I do this stuff?

Amy Clegg (11)
Didsbury Road Primary School

My Little Brother

I hate my little brother,
He really is a pest,
But my mad father
Is always saying he's the best.

I hate my little brother,
He really gets me down,
But still my father likes him,
I really don't see why.

I hate my little brother,
He screams and bites me,
But I love my brother
And he loves me.

Elizabeth Smith (11)
Didsbury Road Primary School

MY DREAM GARDEN

If I could have a garden
I know how it would be,
They'd be daisies and buttercups
And an apple tree.

A dog would chase a ball there,
A bird would sit and sing
And a little cat would play with
A little piece of string.

There would be willow trees
Hanging over wild plants
And I would get rid of
All the dead ants.

There'd be caterpillars
Crawling across the ground,
The bees would collect pollen,
But mother bee would be crowned

And in the very middle,
I'd only have to stand,
For ladybirds and butterflies
To settle on my hand.

Louise Ellis (11)
Didsbury Road Primary School

THE SLY FOX

The sly fox goes rummaging . . . rummaging
He went through the bins
And prowled the garden
He crept up the drives
And scared away the birds

He . . . makes a lot of noise
He wakes up the boys
He hides in his den
Whenever he sees men
The sly fox causes . . . chaos . . . chaos

He jumps through the trees
Even if home to bees
He'd climb on the tables
And upset the cables
The sly fox is very able . . . very able

So he hides in his den
When he sees some men
He upsets cables
And climbs on tables
And he scares away birds
So the sly fox goes rummaging
Have you heard?

Jonathan Edge (10)
Didsbury Road Primary School

SHH, IT'S A SECRET

There were two little girls who knew
All about their evil aunt from Peru
She wakes up at night
Ready to fight
With a terrible knight through and through

The girls have to wake
Just like the boys
To understand why she has to fight
With an evil knight
It's surely, truly awful

Jessica Sharp (10)
Didsbury Road Primary School

THE STORM

The storm trashed the night
Rain pierced down
The wind howled like an abandoned wolf
And the thunder boomed

The dogs barked wildly
The cats miaowed in and out of the night
The owls screeched
And the thunder boomed

The trees swayed as if waving to the storm
The moon a shadow
Clouds clutched the stars like moving hands
And the thunder boomed

The sea crashed like galloping horses
The fields flooded
Lightning slashed the sky like the blade of a knife
And the thunder boomed

The people snuggle in their cosy houses
Marshmallows roasted over the fire
The baby sleeps tucked in bed
And still the thunder booms.

Jack Cargill (10)
Didsbury Road Primary School

The Dolphin

Under the water,
Under the sea,
I've got a special friend waiting for me.

Sleek blue body,
That shines in the sun,
Dappled like moonlight,
Or a white unicorn.

Leaping and diving,
She tumbles and turns,
Without making a sound,
Until the tide turns.

Now the tide's in,
She's hidden in blue,
My friend the dolphin,
Says goodbye to you.

Alexandra Watson (11)
Didsbury Road Primary School

Hollywood

Hollywood, glorious Hollywood
Where all the stars live
Only if I could live in Hollywood
Just imagine the stars I could live with

The sunshine so bright
Always sunshine, never rain
Hollywood, what a sight
In Hollywood there's no violence or pain

I love Hollywood and 20th Century Fox
I love the five star movies
Because I can tell you they're not a
Bunch of sweaty socks

Please let me live in Hollywood
Let me live afar
I really would if I could
Just think, I would live like a star.

Jaydon Jones (10)
Didsbury Road Primary School

ABOUT MY DAD

My dad, my dad,
He is not mad,
He's the very best,
Even though he wears a vest.
I don't think vests are in fashion,
But he seems to have a passion,
He pretends they're really cool,
But he knows they're really drool.
He is so kind,
In his happy mind,
He even lets me stay up late,
But he goes to bed at eight.
His meals are rubbish, he cannot cook,
He has to look in a cookery book,
Overall my dad is ace,
He can even win a race.
He is totally un-mad,
That is him, my special dad.

Bethany Leonard (10)
Didsbury Road Primary School

THE WORLD!

The world is so big
The world is so great
I'm glad I live in this world so great
It has been here since 1988

I love this world
It is so great
How long has it been here?
I think '88

Why is the world so great?
Why is the world so big?
When was it created?
Was it in the 80s?

I need to know when it was created,
I just need to know if it was the 80s,
Please will someone tell me?
Was it in the 80s?

Darriel Booth (11)
Didsbury Road Primary School

DAFFODILS

Daffodils, daffodils
Twinkle like stars
Daffodils, daffodils
Polluted by cars

Daffodils, daffodils
Live in the ground
Daffodils, daffodils
Don't make a sound

Daffodils, daffodils
Dislike strong winds
Daffodils, daffodils
Wish they had wings

Daffodils, daffodils
Like the rest
Daffodils, daffodils
I think they're best!

Rebecka Dalton (10)
Didsbury Road Primary School

WHO INVENTED SCHOOL?

Who invented school?
Whose idea was it?
If I had met them,
I'd say stop it!

Who invented school?
Who invented maths?
Who invented English
And those terrible SATs?

Who invented school?
Who invented art?
Who invented teachers,
Trying to make us smart?

Who invented school?
Who invented my pen?
Who invented my pencil?
I'll never forgive them!

Chris Hand (10)
Didsbury Road Primary School

IF I WAS A ...

If I was a ball,
I would bounce around the hall.

If I was a cat,
I would have to sleep on a mat.

If I was a car,
I would polish it like a star.

If I was a daisy,
I would be so lazy.

If I was a bed,
I would have to be the head.

But I think being me,
It's better than all the rest,
So I'm the *best!*

Thomas Slevin (11)
Didsbury Road Primary School

MY SISTER

My sister lives inside her room,
She dances with a big brown broom.

No one knows what it looks like,
But if you go in, you might go, 'Yikes!'

It could be yellow with big pink spots,
It could have the flu or chicken pox.

You can smell the odour from downstairs,
It smells like rotting purple pears.

I don't dare to go inside,
Because I might not come out alive.

So I'll never see my sister's room,
Or her dancing with the broom.

Amy Gill (10)
Didsbury Road Primary School

FOOD FIGHT

A jam sandwich flies through the air
The dinner ladies stand and stare
The tables are over
And so are the chairs
The war has started, *food fight!*

A sausage flies, a lump of cheese
And don't forget the mushy peas
On the spoons
And away they flew
The war has started, *food fight!*

A custard tart hits the teacher in the face
And then begins the human race
Back go the tables
Back go the chairs
The war has ended, *phew!*

Lauren McCullough (10)
Didsbury Road Primary School

SCHOOL KIDS

Boys, boys, girls, girls,
Girls wear their hair in curls,
Boys always love Man City,
When girls think they're really pretty.

Boys are really sporty,
When girls are naughty,
Teachers shout about,
While their backs are stout.

Boys, boys, girls, girls,
Boys and girls hate their dinner,
So they throw it in the bin
And think they're a winner.

Boys think they're cool,
Girls think they're top of the school,
Teachers get witty,
When kids wander into their own city.

Girls always shop,
When boys think they're top,
So once again,
Boys, boys, girls, girls.

Girls wear their hair in curls,
Boys always love Man City,
When girls think they're pretty,
But of course, are they in their own world?

Becky Parker (11)
Didsbury Road Primary School

THE PERILOUS PIRANHA

Under the ocean, the deep blue sea
That is where you'll find me
I swim and I munch
And I give a hard firm punch
I am a perilous piranha

My worst enemy is up on land
With two helping hands
He's got his net and harpoon
I really hate him, he's a baboon
I am a perilous piranha

He caught my friends
I think he's round the bend
He lost his marbles, he surely did
But now he has a stupid kid
I am a perilous piranha

He's finally dead
Wahoo, I can go to bed
But what's this I see?
No, it mustn't be
I am a perilous piranha

It's his son, back for more
This is going to be a bore
He's got a harpoon and a net
I think I'll win, that's a bet
I am a perilous piranha.

Steven Galloway (11)
Didsbury Road Primary School

MY ALPHABET CLASS

A is Amy, Adam and Ashley,
B is Bob, Bart and Bill,
C is Carol, Catherine and Colin,
D is David, Dill and Daisy,
E is Eric, Evan and Ellis,
F is Faye, Francine and Frank,
G is Ginny, Gary and Gareth,
H is Harry, Hannah and Harriet,
I is Isabel, Izzy and Igna,
J is Jack, Jill and Joshua,
K is Kate, Kenny and Kirk,
L is Lucy, Luke and Lucinda,
M is Mary, Mike and Melanie,
N is Norman, Nicky and Nick,
O is Oliver, Oscar and Olivia,
P is Percy, Penny and Polly,
Q is Quepy, Quankey and Queeny,
R is Richard, Rebecca and Rose,
S is Sam, Sammy and Samantha,
T is Tim, Tom and Thomas,
U is Ula, Uleen and Uzma,
V is Vicky, Victoria and Velma,
W is Wesley, Wilson and William,
X is Xleen, Xtan and Xter,
Y is Yan, Yasaad and Yaneen,
Z is Zoe, Zeeber and Zara.

Rachel Young (10)
Didsbury Road Primary School

MY FAMILY

One of my sisters always goes out,
While the house is left in a mess,
Before she goes out,
We make it less of a mess,
So my mum isn't in a stress.

My other sister has some friends round,
They stay inside with not a dance or a shout,
Until, from upstairs, I hear a loud sound,
One of her friends is standing there,
They'd been dancing again!

My mum sits in the living room,
With a glass of wine
And all she can hear is . . .
Boom! Boom! Boom!
'Turn it down,' she says with a frown.

My dad is cool,
He drives around in a sports car,
He's not much of a fool,
But he always says, 'Ta!'
At least he doesn't drool.

Then there's me,
Plain old me,
I have a good family,
Sometimes they're strange,
But at least they're there for me!

Lauren Thorpe (10)
Didsbury Road Primary School

UNITED WE STAND

Ha ha, the sheep go *baa*
City lose because they're bad news
Even though they've won the game,
They still get relegated once again,
Whilst United are at the top,
City drop down, down, down,
A few weeks later at the finals,
United have won the European Cup,
Also the Premier League too,
So whilst City watch in shame,
United celebrate once again,
A few years later at the local derby,
City lose, that's good news,
Believe me, you don't want to know the score.

Liam Whelan (10)
Didsbury Road Primary School

TIME

When your wheel is spun
Your time on Earth has begun
There are many obstacles in your path
And they will slow you down
And when your wheel stops
You are torn away

It won't matter how long you have
It is how you use it.

Alex Bolland (11)
Didsbury Road Primary School

MY DAD

My dad's cool but he usually drools
Even though he bought me a swimming pool
My dad is really, really cool

My dad's cool, it's really, really true
But sometimes he can make a noise like moo
I really hate it, I really, really do
So I buy him a new pair of shoes
But still my dad's really, really cool

My dad's annoying, he gets on my nerves
Because last week he brought in lots of birds
Even though he's the best, he also beats the rest
And he's still my favourite dad
But will always be really, really cool.

Joshua Harrison (10)
Didsbury Road Primary School

SCHOOL DINNERS

Mustard, custard, chips and peas,
Pick up a plate and move along please.

Biscuits, cake, jelly, ice cream,
This kind of food won't make you lean.

Hotdogs, soups and lovely hotpot,
But watch your tongue, it might be too hot.

Come to our school for your school dinners,
Because they are definite winners!

Rachel Lennie (10)
Didsbury Road Primary School

FIREWORKS

Catherine wheels spin round and round,
Making a squealing, whizzing sound.

Rockets shoot up in the sky,
Like an astronaut waving goodbye.

Sparklers fizz like a stick on fire,
You wave them around and they get higher and higher.

Shooting stars fly through space,
Out of all the fireworks they're ace.

When the fireworks are in the action,
They soon become the main attraction.

Felicia Farrimond (11)
Didsbury Road Primary School

THE COWARDLY KING OF THE BEASTS

The king of the beasts is scared of a dog,
He is scared of a cat and also a frog.

The king of the beasts is scared of a snail,
He is scared of an ant and also a whale.

The king of the beasts is scared of a mouse,
He is scared of a bird and also a house.

But people say, why is he scared of a house?
Because all those animals live in the house,
Especially the mouse.

Chloe Lowry (10)
Didsbury Road Primary School

JUMPING JACK

J umping, jumping, it is great,
U nder, over, up and down, do a roly-poly and smack on the ground,
M y name is Jumping Jack, I jump every day,
P ing-pong, ding-dong-do,
I have a sister called Moo.
N o, no, you're jumping all wrong,
G o like this and then sing along,

J umping, jumping, it is great,
A fish like you should be able to jump a mile or two,
C ause you're young, I'll let you off with a warning,
K ick that little tail of yours so I can deal with you in the morning.

Molly Temperley-Cassin (10)
Didsbury Road Primary School

ON MY STREET

I was walking down my street and I was about to see,
My oldest mate, David but he hadn't seen me,
He fell over and I ran to him,
He was OK but he had a limp,
We were walking around and we went to his house,
As soon as we got in we went and looked at his mouse,
After that we went to the couch
And turned on the TV and saw Papa Roach,
After that I decided to go home and go to bed,
But I mustn't forget to take my ted.

Ben Jolley (11)
Didsbury Road Primary School

BLUE

Under the sea
Under the bright-blue sky
Inside the dull-blue folder

Was a magnificent long multicoloured fish
It swam slowly, it swam fast
It made a fool of itself in front of its class

I don't know why he did it, he must be mad
I wouldn't do it, that's for sure

Under the sea
Under the bright-blue sky
Inside the dull-blue folder.

Nicola Brennan (10)
Didsbury Road Primary School

BASKETBALL

B asketball is my favourite sport
A nd I am always on the same court
S o I always get a basket three times
K icking is not allowed
E ven my friend is cool
T wo, one, zero
B asketball was over
A ll our team won the match
L ots of people were clapping
L ots of adults were happy.

Matthew Hartley (10)
Didsbury Road Primary School

MY BIRDS

Birds, birds
With a capital B
You're so cute and furry
You're the ones for me
A tweet-tweet here
And a tweet-tweet there
While you fly around everywhere

Birds, birds
With a capital B
You're so small and tiny
With a capital T
You sleep all day
And eat your food
You're so cute and tiny
You're the ones for me.

Asadullah Haider (11)
Didsbury Road Primary School

FOOTBALL

F   ootball is great and I really like it
O   h I like it so much and I'm so fit
O   h I hate it when dogs come on the pitch
T   ennis is great but football is better
B   ut I'm a good footballer so I wear my sweater
A   nd I score all the time, so I'm so fine
L   ook at me scoring my goal, sometimes I eat out of a big bowl
L   ife would be rubbish if there were no goals.

Leon King (10)
Didsbury Road Primary School

MY FRIEND

My friend keeps me high when I am so down
She always comforts me when I am alone
There's no need for saying how dreadful it is
To fall out and break up, I won't say it's bliss!

I hope we'll be friends forever and ever
Our hearts are attached like one when we're together
She's up for a laugh, whatever the weather
Even if she's not that clever!

So now you know that friends make the world go round
That they'll always be there for you, they'll always be around
So that's what friends are always for
And hopefully I'll make some more.

Tammy Aldawery (10)
Didsbury Road Primary School

THE MIGHTY SHARK

As I swim and I dive
To the bottom of the sea
There's a whale and a piranha waving at me.
There's catfish, tropical fish,
Fish with no nose
Hey, there's a glamour fish
Striking a pose.
It's a great little city
Where fish play in the park
But I'm the king; the mighty shark.

David Hayes (11)
Didsbury Road Primary School

THE SKY AT NIGHT

When I look at the sky at night
I always wonder why the stars twinkle like a light
Above our heads
And through the sky

When I look at the sky at night
I always wonder why the moon shines really bright
And makes light
All of the night

When I look at the sky at night
I always wonder why the stars twinkle
And the moon shines
Oh well
Never mind.

Yasmin Cooper (10)
Didsbury Road Primary School

THE MYSTERY

Mumble of a word goes far
Is it the mystery or is it sky high
In that great blue sky?
Ron should know
Do you know about the mystery not quite solved?
I give tips, so I will give you one
Don't go in my attic
You might blow my cover.

Pepy Wilson (11)
Didsbury Road Primary School

THE BRIGHTENING

The door opened, creaking; fairies scared,
Something big, tall and angry,
The royal empress with her scary and chilling embrace,
Battle between good and evil desolating,
Fairies hiding, giants come,
Could this be the end for some?
Ghost flying, scouting the fort,
Thunder, a ground-shaking crash like an earthquake.
Gentle tiptoeing all around the room,
Danger! Danger! High voltage.
Giants everywhere.
There was no time to stand and stare,
They see somebody over there.
Somebody goes but nobody shows,
Just the ghosts playing tricks,
But one gets caught, they all start to flee,
Killed one by one, wings crushed and tails buried.
But something's coming,
Big, strong and almighty,
The force of good had come to brighten the day.

Aidan Morris (11)
Forest Park School

GNOMES AND GIANTS

As the moon came up over the eerie wood
Loud screams could be heard in the air,
As the giant of the mountain came for blood
In search of a gnome to snare.

The earth began to tremble and shake
As the giant began to search,
The poor little gnomes began to quake
And hid in the bole of a birch.

The giant could tell by the scent on the breeze
That the gnomes were somewhere around,
But then the giant gave a mighty sneeze
And collapsed in a heap on the ground.

Matthew Vernon (11)
Forest Park School

THE GETAWAY

As the fairies run and run
The goblins aim with their gun
The fairies hide beneath the trees
Scattering around like bumblebees

One of the goblins called Arty Marty
Organised a big search party
As the fairies fly oh so high
So high that they can reach the sky

The goblins cannot climb that much
So they give up and go back to their hutch
But in their hutch they're not so happy
They need a plan and make it snappy

They plan and scheme a great ambush
So at the fairies they can rush
And then they'll steal their powers of old
And take away their fairy gold

But goblins you had better beware
The fairies are waiting in their lair
Don't forget that they're not dumb
And can easily deal with goblin scum.

Sean Savage (11)
Forest Park School

THE GNOME

Small people running, running
Evil gnomes chasing, chasing.
Started a chase around and around.
Small people hiding under the stairs,
Footsteps, stamping round the castle,
Bang!
Someone waking, heard a rattle,
Danger! Danger!
The gnomes escape.

Someone waking,
Tiptoeing,
Sneaking around
. . . Then running,
Charging, charging,
Faster and faster,
. . . Then stop.
Got them cornered.
Scary, chilling, menacing,
A ghost.
Then a scream,
That was the last of the team.

Amy McGuire (10)
Forest Park School

THE GOBLINS AND THE GIANTS

As the goblins run and run,
Giants come to have some fun.
Goblins scatter everywhere,
Like pieces of glass over there.

As the goblins rush and rush,
The giants come and have some fun.
As they plod and plod and bump around,
Like marbles scattering on the ground.

Callum Tipper (11)
Forest Park School

THE GNOME

Giants running,
Gnomes are running,
Tiptoe,
Tiptoe,
Giants hunt the gnomes,
Giants find the gnomes,
Giants running,
Gnomes are running,
Trapped in a corner,
There's no escape,
Danger,
Danger,
Tiptoe,
Tiptoe,
The giants looking,
The giants searching,
Hunts them,
Finds them,
Giants running,
Gnomes are running,
Gnomes are trapped,
Gnomes don't escape.

Natalie Graham (10)
Forest Park School

GOBLINS AND FAIRIES

Sneaking slowly through the undergrowth,
Green, pale goblins walking slowly, slowly,
Menacing, big and strong, hardy and bloodthirsty,
Goblins sneak from tree to tree,
They hide behind them for the good.

Tinkle, tinkle go the bells of the fairies,
Wings fluttering, good old fairies fly
The path through the forest of darkness,
Dressed with silk and lace they fly
Through the forest of death.

Haunting voices the fairies hear,
Growling, grunting, must be goblins,
Run, fly, get away fairies,
Before the goblins get you,
Too late, fairies perish under the evil minions of the dark,
Under the evil minions of the dark.

Christopher Duncan (11)
Forest Park School

THE TROLL AND THE GNOME

The castle walls shake and quiver
A shadow looms against the tower
The gnome scampers down the steps
And the troll drags his club behind.

You see the troll is awfully jealous
Of the gnome's good looks,
Oh, how he wishes it was he who had
Those yellow eyes and that grey beard
And the great big wart on his nose.

The troll raises his club to strike
But finds that the little creature is nowhere in sight
And then the gnome calls from the window,
'I have had a good day, bad sir, but now I say goodnight,
For now I shall escape with my magical power of flight!'

Alex Warden (11)
Forest Park School

THE GNOME

The gnome tiptoeing behind, sneaking away.
Then stamp, stamp, stamp a giant comes.
The gnome tries to escape then . . .
A giant tries to fight the gnome.
In the haunted castle where no one will survive.
A ghost comes to scare,
But he cannot even bear, 'Ooo!' the ghost whispers,
Trying to scare although he had no hair.

A fairy wakes up
She tiptoes downstairs,
Twinkle, twinkle she goes.
Sneaking, hiding to see what was there.
All she could see was,
'Danger, danger, danger.'

The gnome comes up to the fairy,
Suddenly *crash, bash, clash, bash, clatter, shatter,*
The giant kills the gnome.
The ghost runs as fast as he can.
Then strolling, rolling, tumbling, the ghost never came back,
The giant became friends forever with the tiny fairy.

Sonia Kaur Bamrah (10)
Forest Park School

AUTUMN LEAVES

I see orange, red and golden leaves twirling exactly
Like a tornado doing somersaults all over the place,
You see them flying gracefully, falling gently on the ground,
Burgundy, red, yellow, scarlet and crimson,
Beautiful colours, the leaves dance like acrobats.

When I jump, I hear them crunching, making funny noises,
Sometimes I wish it was my comfortable bed,
Rustling, swishing you hear,
Crackling you hear and you want to kick it desperately.

Some feel damp, some are dry, some feel crispy and brittle, soggy,
Some feel prickly and bumpy, others feel spongy and smooth,
They smell like a summer's day is coming towards the world.

Nikhil Parmar (8)
Forest Park School

FROST

The crystal shining ice melts on the cars,
Crystal shining ice melts on cars.
It then changes its home to the gardens and roads,
Changes its home to roads and gardens.
It's just like ice cream, melting in your hand,
Melting in your hand, eating ice cream.
Don't forget to tell people not to slip on the ice,
A warning, not to slip.
Just when everyone gets to work and school,
The sun comes out to brighten the day,
Just as children go off to school and play.

Nathan Lindo (11)
Forest Park School

AUTUMN POEM

All is dark in the sleek evening sky
and migrating birds have flown by.
Under the trees lie the fallen plums,
a feast for wasps and all their chums.
The autumn leaves turn magenta and cold,
coating the floor with a carpet of gold.
Up in the trees the apples are due,
a tasty apple pie for me and you.
Monsters and ghouls knock at your door
and their costumes scare you to the core.
Nuts are gathered for the squirrel's store
and autumn falls like a blanket once more.

Henry Mills (8)
Forest Park School

FIREWORKS

Boom! The rocket explodes in the air
sending colourful rain to the ground.
Screech! The screechers shoot up into the air,
stars falling like rain.
The crackling sparklers sparkle like mad,
you can make patterns with this glittering wand.
Whoosh! The Catherine wheel whizzes round,
making a little popping sound.
Snap! Crash! Bang! Roman candles sending a
rainbow of colours into the atmosphere.

Elliott Davis (8)
Forest Park School

THE GNOME

Sneaking, sneaking quietly,
Tiptoe, tiptoe as we go,
Chasing, chasing, run, run and run,
Lion chasing his prey,
Sneaking around, don't get cornered.
There he is, get him,
Get him now!
Corner him *now!*
Turn around, he has gone.
You have not got me now, I've run away,
Up the railings should I go?
Not really, I'll go out of the front door.

Katie Skinkis (10)
Forest Park School

WINTER TREES

The roots twisting under the ground,
searching for water like octopus' tentacles.
The trunk all knobbly on each side
bent like an old man's back.
The branches swaying in the winter wind
reaching, reaching to touch the sky.
The twigs snapping like witch's fingers
trying to grab you.
All the branches covered with a blanket of glittering,
gleaming, glistening snow, sparkling in the sun.

Lauren Pye (8)
Forest Park School

WINTER

Wind that blows in your face
snow that follows behind
Ice forming into snowflakes
snowflakes forming snow
Nothing but soft, white gleaming snow
against the navy-blue sky
Thick white blanket
spread across the ground
Every star twinkling in the night sky
thousands and thousands form pictures
Robins dig in the snow
looking for food.

Rachel Robinson (9)
Forest Park School

THE GIANT'S CASTLE

The chase between good and evil
Gnomes, fairies and elves,
Chasing down stairs and through secret passages,
In the giant's castle.
Then the sleepy giant wakes,
He treads hungrily and menacingly,
Stomp, stomp, stomp,
Hearing a fairy, elf and gnome.
Then the gallant three are gone,
Gone, under the giant's foot.

Jack McGuire (11)
Forest Park School

THE GIANT AND THE GNOME

The tiny gnome, scattering, scattering,
trying to find a hiding place.
The huge giant is looking for a gnome,
with an angry look on his face.

Listen, listen,
to the shivering bushes,
seeing the giant,
the gnome rushes.

Rushing, rushing,
he tries to escape,
but the giant catches up,
Danger!

The poor little gnome, panting, panting,
trying to race on.
The hungry giant, stamping, stamping,
the gnome's breath was gone.

Suddenly he tripped and fell to the ground,
now he is hurt and sure to be found.

The gnome was caught
and taken away,
the giant had finally
captured his prey.

Jessica Foley (10)
Forest Park School

MY MAGIC BOX
(Based on the poem 'Magic Box' by Kit Wright)

I will put in my box . . .

A swirl of silk on a summer's night,
A breeze from the coldest countries,
Fire from a fierce fighting dragon.

I will put in my box . . .

A twinkle from the brightest star,
A spark from a fire,
The oldest piece of cotton.

I will put in my box . . .

A last word from an Egyptian,
The first gurgle from a baby,
The last hackle from a witch.

My box is fashioned by . . .

The bluest water,
The hinges are made from the oldest wood,
The lid is fashioned with gold gems,
I shall sunbathe in my box on the golden sands,
Then float away in a boat.

My box is special.

Katie Johnson (9)
Golborne CP School

OUR MAGIC BOX
(Based on the poem 'Magic Box' by Kit Wright)

We will put in our box . . .
A yellow sea and a blue sun,
With a jumping joker telling jokes
And a cowboy with a humorous gun.

We will put in our box . . .
Hair from your nose and a nose on your head,
With a pop group always rapping,
Bouncing balls delighting the crowd.

We will put in our box . . .
Enchanted secrets never told,
Conversations open to all,
Stories told that are never-ending.

We will play football in our box
And always win our own matches,
Scoring in every match.

Our box is made out of chocolate,
With sweets for its hinges,
Icing over the handles
And ice mints for a lock.

Amy Lally (9)
Golborne CP School

OUR MAGIC BOX
(Based on the poem 'Magic Box' by Kit Wright)

We will put in our box . . .
A yellow sea and a blue sun,
With a jumping joker telling jokes
And a cowboy with a humorous gun.

We will put in our box . . .
Hair from your nose and a nose on your head,
With a pop group always rapping,
Bouncing balls delighting the crowd.

We will put in our box . . .
Enchanted secrets never told,
Conversations open to all,
Stories told that are never-ending.

We will play football in our box
And always win our own matches,
Scoring in every match.

Our box is made out of chocolate,
With sweets for its hinges,
Icing over the handles
And ice mints for a lock.

Emily Prior (9)
Golborne CP School

My Magic Box
(Based on the poem 'Magic Box' by Kit Wright)

I will put in my box . . .

A cowboy in a car
And a driver on a horse.
A fish in a field
And a sheep in a lake.

I will put in my box . . .

A cow on a broomstick
And a witch in a barn.
A cat with a rumbling stomach,
The first joke of an uncle.

My box is fashioned of wood, metal and gold,
There are mysteries in the corners of my box,
Its hinges are gold.

I shall skate in my box,
On the high hills of Africa,
I shall surf in the warm Atlantic water.

Anthony Heesom (9)
Golborne CP School

My Magic Box
(Based on the poem 'Magic Box' by Kit Wright)

I will put in the box . . .
Shiny rings and millions of necklaces,
The tip of a tongue of a Chinese dragon,
A sip of some water from the shiniest sea.
I will put in the box . . .
A girl as an army man and a man as a ballet dancer,
End of another alphabet.

I will put in the box . . .
A sprinkle of the Atlantic Ocean,
A dark day and a bright night,
A white sun and a yellow moon.

My box is fashioned in the way of a cube,
It is shiny and it has secrets in each corner.

I will use my box so that I can sail and go to sunny places.

Craig Dale (9)
Golborne CP School

MY MAGIC BOX
(Based on the poem 'Magic Box' by Kit Wright)

I will put in my magic box . . .

A necklace made from a tooth of a shark,
A bear in a bus,
A boy in an ark.

I will put in my box . . .

The glistening light from outer space,
The darkness of the sun
And a turtle trying to race.

My box is fashioned from diamonds to gleaming gold,
With a marvellous marbled crystal ball,
Predicting what the future holds.

In my box, I shall surf with the luscious dolphins,
Do gymnastics on the clouds.
My box is truly special,
I think it's unique alone.

Shauna Woodward (9)
Golborne CP School

SCHOOL RULES!

School rules are boring
And all of us are yawning
Do we have to get up in the morning?
Because school is far too boring!

Time for us to go, but the rules say no, no, no
But we just go.
The next day we can't go out to play
And it's the best part of the day!
Oh, what will we do?
I should not have got up in the morning!
Morning is near, I said, 'I can't hear,'
But Mum kicked me out of bed!
So once again I'm in pain,
For lying and for going to boring old school!
Playtime's here, everyone cheers,
The rules shout, we rush out
And the rules burst into tears!
Holidays are here, we cheer,
The rules stop talking, we run out to play!

Joanna Steele (9)
Great Moor Junior School

A SHINY NEW PENNY

I'm a shiny new penny
The new kid on the block
I wonder where my home will be
A purse, a wallet, an old sock?
I'm fired up with adventure
I want to make my mark
I'm going to see the world
Maybe the cinema, the shops, even the park

I don't need a lot to keep me happy
A snugly pocket will do
I only want my new owner
To take me sometimes to the zoo
If you're ever looking at a new penny
Don't be in a hurry to spend
If I stay long enough
I could be your very best friend!

Faye Drinkwater (9)
Great Moor Junior School

SCHOOL

School is boring, all you do is work,
The teachers shout at you,
Maths is dead easy,
English is easier,
Science is rubbish,
All you do is sit there and write,
How boring is that to you?
Someone throws a rubber and they blame it on you.
We get a trip once every three years,
All we do there is sit down and look at the worst paintings in the world,
Our teacher gets stressed out because of the people being naughty.
My best friend was sick, the teacher blamed me
Because I'm his best friend,
When we got back to school, we did maths,
The teacher asked us 2x2,
Someone shouted 4,
Then I go, 'We're in year 5 you know,'
I go to the head teacher, he's that dense he sneezes and goes,
'Hullabaloo!'

Joe Garnett (10)
Great Moor Junior School

SAD DAYS AND HAPPY DAYS

On a cold September day,
A car hit Sooty straight away,
He only lived for two weeks,
He was buried under a tree,
But forever in my heart with me.

The next day was quite a shock,
My dad bought Molly,
Molly is a good cat,
Nearly the best,
But nothing could replace Sooty.

I imagine Sooty in the sky,
Playing a harp
Or singing a lullaby,
But forever in my heart with me.

Jodhi Taylor (10)
Great Moor Junior School

THE LOST LITTLE KITTEN

I am a little kitten,
Sad to say,
While I am walking on my way,
Searching around for food to eat,
Always being stamped on
By people's big feet
I look through people's window at the other cats,
Eating lots of biscuits and playing with rubber bats
And just look at me,

I look like a rag,
When I was smaller I lived in a bag,
But my life changed, a little girl came
And after all that I was never the same.
I lived with the girl that saved my life,
She gave me food and chopped it with a knife.
Now I live with lots of kittens
And I am another, but I will still
Love my dead lovely mother.

Heather Waterhouse (9)
Great Moor Junior School

SCHOOL

I come to school every morning,
Half asleep and I'm still yawning.
Go through the entrance hall,
Hear all the teachers start to call,
Class 7, class 8, class 9.

Our teacher's called Miss S,
She really hates a mess.
So if you keep things tidy,
She won't be such a snidy.

When there's trouble, she'll be there,
It's not as if she doesn't care.
She can be quite kind
And when you're naughty,
She sometimes doesn't mind.

Bradley Webb (9)
Great Moor Junior School

SPACE ANIMAL

If a hamster went to space,
He'd surely pull a face.
If he met a cat, he'd run for his life
And if he met a dog, that cat would be a kitten.
But if he got a lion, teeth like knives,
He'd run like a mitten.
He'd come back with a pack of wolves
And the lion would run for his life,
But if this hamster said *woof,*
His little life would be shorter.

The fools had killed themselves for an oil spillage,
Set off an explosion,
What happened then? They died,
Hooray!

Jonathan Bramwell (9)
Great Moor Junior School

FOOTBALL CRAZY!

Football, I play it every day,
Home or away.

In rain, even if it is a pain,
I play football every day.

Football, I play it every day,
In snow all day.

I play it in shorts,
Even if it is cold.

Oh, I play it every day.

Daniel Banfield (9)
Great Moor Junior School

This Is The News Of Two Girls

This is the news of two girls,
They went on a picnic to see some shoes,
The shoes said, 'Yo.'
They put them on.
Those two girls walked for 200 days,
They saw some sparrows up above,
They shot those from up above
Because they poohed in their hair
And ate those sparrows from up above.
Two helicopters came and rescued the girls,
The girls they rescued were very ill,
They died the next day,
Because of the excitement of the *hullabaloo!*

Alex Hopkins (10)
Great Moor Junior School

Turtle

The turtle is a clever chap,
Oh how he wishes he could nap,
Then one day he plays a prank,
But does not rob the bank.

He goes into a joke shop
And buys himself some skates,
Watch out, here he comes,
He's skating into gates.
Suddenly he has a lot of mates.

Ellie Gaffney (9)
Great Moor Junior School

A Riddle Can Rhyme

This riddle can rhyme,
It's so boring,
You might as well be yawning.
The teachers are roaring at the boy
Who was naughty,
The children are under 40.
The playground is where you have fun,
We won the game,
I know your name.
You play for Apollo,
I bet you lose tomorrow.
If you're not home by ten-past three,
You'll be late for tea.

Aaron Upton (9)
Great Moor Junior School

The Murderer

The round moon beamed on the grassy floor
And I ran on further more,
The sky was black as ink,
I tried to run while I tried to think,
The slow tickle on my face was frightening,
I couldn't breathe,
I couldn't see,
I tripped and cut my knee,
He came up to me and stabbed me in the heart,
Suddenly I felt cold, my life had been sold.

Benjamin Johnson (10)
Great Moor Junior School

DRIP DROP

Drip drop
Sit on my lap, going down the drainpipe
Hit my head
Don't know where I'm going
Going up the drainpipe
Going down the drainpipe
Smack my head
Don't know where I'm going
Where's the drip coming from?
And there it goes again
Drip drop, drip drop
Oh no, hit my head
Going down the drainpipe
Where's that drip coming from?

Claire Carr (9)
Great Moor Junior School

SCHOOL

The clock's ticking
Teacher's going mad
There's absolutely no fun to be had
Tick, tock, tick, tock

Five minutes till home time
Bell's about to chime
The chocolate biscuit at home is mine
Tick, tock, tick, tock . . . *brrring*

We all shout, 'Hurray,'
At last it's the end of the day.

Ruby McLean (9)
Great Moor Junior School

MY GREAT AUNTIE

My great auntie, she is dead,
She died from loneliness in a hospital bed.
She needed a drip but she said no,
She lay there day after day.
A couple of days later, nurses found her,
Laid on her bed,
One of the nurses said,
'She is happy in her long, long sleep,
No more pain for her.'
But I still miss her so.
In September or October is when she died,
But whenever it happened I still miss my Karin.
But she is here with me, but as a ghost,
She is helping me get through this day,
My great auntie, she is dead,
She died of loneliness in a hospital bed.

Helen Giles (10)
Great Moor Junior School

HOME TIME

When time is ticking, I hope it's home time,
Can't wait 'til it's home time.
I can imagine what's happening in the future,
When I get home, I'm always right.
I wish I could fast-forward time,
It would be the greatest gift I'd have.
When I'd get home, I'd be playing on my Xbox
Or maybe reading horrible histories.

Freddie McCoy (9)
Great Moor Junior School

TEACHERS

Teachers are from the land of work,
Devils as they smirk,
Asking you lots of questions,
Handing out lots of detentions.
That's a teacher!
Telling you what to do,
Getting away from them is yahoo!
Giving homework out all the time,
Not let you go and dine.
That's a teacher!
Even worse than your mum,
Never letting you play the drum,
Every second expecting you to sit up straight,
But they just can't wait,
That's a teacher!

Joe Graham (9)
Great Moor Junior School

CUP OF THE YEAR

Cup of the year
Gold cups are very dear
Let's try and win this year
Last year
When a deer
Came and blocked the winning shot
Of the year
The ball came back off the deer
Hit me in the ear, went in the goal
That was the winning goal of the year.

Matthew Cookson (9)
Great Moor Junior School

WORLD WAR II

Bombs are falling
How boring
Machine guns are firing
People are crying
Why are people dying?
Falling bombs

More people are dying
Sergeants are lying
Grenades are flying
Trees are falling
Sergeants are calling
Even more boring.

Michael Booth (9)
Great Moor Junior School

THE MOON

The moon shimmers
like a disco ball
    flickers
like a bright shining candle
    glides
like a swift man on skis
    spins
like a colourful merry-go-round
    dangles
like a bright silver yo-yo on a piece of string
    glimmers
like a crystal cave in the sky.

Frances Reilly (9)
Holy Family RC Primary School

WHO AM I?

Neither hiss nor sting have I
But I have a good home
And I am loved, loved, loved!

Neither human nor skin have I
But I can eat and drink
And I am loved, loved, loved!

Neither trunk nor long tail have I
But I can sleep all day
And I am loved, loved, loved!

For I master every moment
I get exercise on my wheel
And I am loved, loved, loved!

(Hamster)

Rebecca O'Brien (9)
Holy Family RC Primary School

THE MOON

The moon glows
Like a new glimmering diamond
Smiles
Like a welcoming friend
Ticks
Like a clock on a coal-black wall
Spins
Like a gliding, empty merry-go-round
Glimmers
Like a silver coin
Glitters
Like a crystal in sunlight.

Laura Gardener (9)
Holy Family RC Primary School

WHO AM I?

Neither legs nor arms have I
But I dance in the mud
And I
Wiggle, wiggle, wiggle

Neither hands nor feet have I
But I give soil to the Earth
And I
Wiggle, wiggle, wiggle

I master every movement
For I dig and dig
And I
Wiggle, wiggle, wiggle.

(Worm)

Michael Ranson (9)
Holy Family RC Primary School

THE MOON

The moon glides
Like a massive bird soaring through the sky
Glows
Like a spooky flashlight on a dark wall
Whirls
Like an enormous flying saucer
Shoots
Like a huge, silver rocket
Flickers
Like a broken television
Dances
Like a bright disco with people dancing.

Saul Cooper (9)
Holy Family RC Primary School

WHO AM I?

Neither hands nor feet have I
But I tear with my teeth
And I can
Swim, swim, swim

Neither wings nor sting have I
But I have gigantic jaws
And I can
Swim, swim, swim

Neither spit or beak have I
But I attack very bad
And I can
Swim, swim, swim

I master every movement
For I jump, swim and bite
And I can
Swim, swim, swim.

(Shark)

Laurence Francis (8)
Holy Family RC Primary School

YOU HAVEN'T

Tut, tut, you haven't finished your work.
Tut, tut, you haven't finished your washing.

Tut, tut, you haven't gone to bed.
Tut, tut, you're watching your TV.

Sh, sh, I hear the telephone ring.
Bling, bling, have you seen my diamond ring?

Lauren O'Brien (10)
Holy Family RC Primary School

BLUE

Blue as Laura's eyes who I sit next to
Blue as the ruler that I am using
Blue as the pencil pot in front of me
Blue as Lucy's tears who also sits next to me
Blue as the aquarium that I go to
Blue as the light sky that's above me
Blue as the relaxing ocean that I go in.

Megan Comerford (10)
Penketh South Primary School

A JOURNEY HOME

I can see the rabbits
Through the poppies,
The soldiers marching on,
The boat for England is almost gone.
I know that it went on for so long,
But now, thank goodness, it's gone,
The sun still shines on.

Katherine Stephenson (9)
Penketh South Primary School

YELLOW IS...

Yellow is the bright yellow paper.
Yellow is the blazing sun shining down on me.

Yellow is a fluffy chick only 5 weeks old.
Yellow is a ripe banana ready to eat.

Yellow is a lemon too sour for me to eat.
Yellow is a piece of cheese nice and tasty.

Yellow is my pencil case nice and soft.
Yellow is my favourite colour, which makes me nice and warm.

Lauren Hoey (10)
Penketh South Primary School

PEACOCK

Peacock, feathers like a rainbow
Peacock, ink glowing in the sunlight
Peacock, slow and silent
Peacock, a many coloured statue
Peacock, eyes in the feathers
Peacock, oil in a puddle
Peacock, the queen of colours.

April Norton (9)
Penketh South Primary School

SILVER

S oft as feathers
I cy as ice
L ong as a river
V iolent as a shark
E legant as a model
R ed as a rose.

Laura Cupit (10)
Penketh South Primary School

THE OLD TEACHER

When all the children go home,
There's always the old teacher,
Teaching her children,
Shouting, but to you and me silence remains.

Tests are set out,
Slammed on the desks,
Taking the books slowly but silently,
Out of the shelves.

The cleaner arrives cleaning the school,
Does not notice a thing,
Does not hear a thing.

But still the old teacher,
Teaching her remaining children.

Lucy Harrison (9)
Penketh South Primary School

RED IS ...

Red is St George's cross on the England flag on the back of
                                             a travelling car.
Red is the danger that our world possesses.
Red is blood when you get hurt.
Red is the Manchester United shirt.
Red is the circle on the Japanese flag flying in the sky.
Red is the burning fire in my living room keeping me nice and warm.

Calum Anderson (10)
Penketh South Primary School

CUDDLY ANIMALS

Monkeys love to swing through the trees,
Monkeys always love to dance,
Monkeys can never dodge the bees,
Monkeys always lose their pants.

Bunnies never get great hops,
Bunnies have white fluffy tails,
Bunnies can't learn their stops,
Bunnies forget to jump the snails.

Bears are twice the size of a man,
Bears eat a lot of meat,
Bears can squash a can,
Bears have great big feet.

Lions can always pounce,
Lions love to purr,
Lions eat more than an ounce,
Lions never lose their fur.

Kyle Jones (9)
Penketh South Primary School

PLAYING FOOTBALL

Tension building
  Whistles blowing
    Fans cheering
      Flags waving
        Hearts beating
          Someone running
            Beckham kicking
              Owen scoring!

Andrew Smith (8)
Penketh South Primary School

CHEETAH

Cheetah, spotty as a ladybird.
Cheetah, fast as wind.
Cheetah, mad, mysterious monster.
Cheetah, killer of the ground.
Cheetah, gold as treasure.
Cheetah, solid as a rock.

Martyn Driver (9)
Penketh South Primary School

BLUE

Blue is the pen I am writing with at this moment in time.
Blue is the water that comes out of my tap.
Blue is my bedroom wallpaper.
Blue is the sky with not many clouds.
Blue is the hard seat I am sitting on.

Steven Whitfield (10)
Penketh South Primary School

BRICE

There once was a cool penguin called Brice,
Who was terribly, terribly nice,
He just sat there all day,
Couldn't move anyway,
'Cause his bum was just stuck to the ice!

Sarah Gore (8)
Penketh South Primary School

IN THE PLAYGROUND

Hannah playing hide and seek
Tim standing on the line!
Alice screaming and running
Amy feeling fine
Callum with sticky fingers
Jade being a friend
Sophie playing clapping games
Jack starting a trend!
Sara being a butterfly
Hailey dropping crisps!
Daniel and Lloyd sharing break
Children writing lists
But then the bell rings!
All is silent.

Fara Raza (8)
Penketh South Primary School

MY FAVOURITE JOURNEY

A blade of grass, a flower leaf,
A fish below the coral reef.
Winding roads, speeding cars,
People staring right at Mars.
But my favourite journey yet,
Was when I travelled in a jet.
When I got there I was in Spain,
My mum, my dad, me and the pain.
The part of Spain was Benidorm
And then there was a horrid storm.

Joseph Brown (8)
Penketh South Primary School

Yellow Is ...

Yellow is the blazing sun that shines upon the Earth.
Yellow is the runny caramel that sits inside the chocolate.
Yellow is the fluffy chick that's just hatched out the egg.

Yellow is the dancing daffodils that dance just for joy.
Yellow is Winnie the Pooh's body and Tigger's tummy.
Yellow is the sticky honey that Winnie the Pooh eats.

Yellow is a juicy lemon that has just been bitten into.
Yellow is a healthy banana that monkeys love to eat.
Yellow is the ball that bounces on the ground.

Yellow is ...

Kayleigh Kennedy (9)
Penketh South Primary School

Orange

Orange is the horizon when the white stallion gallops across it.
Orange is our spelling books waiting for a good ten out ten!
Orange is the Chinese dragon dancing in the billowing wind.
Orange is the orange juice being carefully poured into the cold glass on the kitchen table.
Orange is the ginger cat licking his lips as he watches the soon to be lifeless mouse scurry across the grass.
Orange is the pencil that is forming this poem.
Orange is the tiger cub playing in the long yellow grass, waiting for his mother to come home, waiting and waiting.

Sadie Kellett (9)
Penketh South Primary School

QUEEN VICTORIA

Q is for Queen Victoria
U is for unique
E is for elegant
E is for everlasting
N is for never giving up

V is for Victoria, her middle name
I is for the ink she wrote in
C is for china dolls, children loved
T is for trappers in those dusty mines
O is for one, the number one queen
R is for raindrops falling from the sky
I is for ice in the winter mall
A is for Alexandrina, the Victorian's queen.

Hayley Croft (8)
Penketh South Primary School

THE LAMPLIGHTER

L is for lamps that he comes to light,
A is for Albert, his name,
M is for money, the jangling in his pocket,
P is for people looking for him.
L is for the lantern that he carries,
I is for impossible, that people think it is,
G is for gardens the he passes,
H is for houses that he sees faces in,
T is for trappers that are walking home,
E is for effort, he puts his effort in it,
R is for rude people pushing him.

Kara-Louise Royle (9)
Penketh South Primary School

CHRISTMAS EVE

C hildren playing with their toys
H ugging parents, making noise
R unning in and out of snow
I ce is hiding, did you know?
S tay by fires, please keep warm
T his is the night that Jesus was born
M ake your Christmas a special one
A ngels sit down, have a scone
S anta's coming, so be good

E verybody's falling with a great big thud
V ests are the thing you really need
E verthing's turning into horrible weeds.

Charlotte Chadwick (9)
Penketh South Primary School

RED IS...

Red is a warm fire blazing with warmness.
Red is the word of danger.
Red is my lovely, carefully-stitched jumper
And the bright lipstick that old elders wear on outings.
Red is the unhappy cross in a boy's maths book.

Red is a colour on a wall.
Red is a sunrise on a calm ocean.
Red is a colour of somebody's face when they are shy
And red is a silky cushion, silky as ever.

Emily Sutton (9)
Penketh South Primary School

LIMERICKS

There once was a lady called Betty,
Who ate a lot of spaghetti,
She married a man,
Whose name was Dan,
Now she's covered in confetti.

There once was a man called Rick,
Who ate a chocolate biscuit,
He ate some more,
His tummy was sore
And now he's feeling quite sick.

Rebecca Green (9)
Penketh South Primary School

RED IS . . .

Red is a roaring fire in the distance coming to get you.
Red is the sun waking up from below the playing fields.
Red is paint on the wall shining in my eyes.
Red is the second hand on the clock going round in a circle.
Red is the box that holds our maths books in it.
Red is a blazing brake light on a car stopping to let people
                                                cross the road.
Red is a danger sign saying not allowed through.
Red is roses ready to be picked.
Red is our jumpers that say Penketh South CP School on them.

Adam Mee (10)
Penketh South Primary School

HORSE

From:
Riding round from C to A
Stacking up your unused hay
Grooming your glossy coat
Feeding you apple and oat

To:
Putting on your tack
Then climbing on your back
And galloping across the horizon
For I am always with you

And now the time has come
To say goodbye
I'm feeling glum
But you are always with me
No matter what.

Rachael Scott (10)
Penketh South Primary School

PLAYING IN WATER

Arms splashing
  Children clapping
    Heavy diving
      Everyone sliding
        Fast swimming
          No drowning!
            Adults moaning
              Swimming ending!

Bethany Bancroft (9)
Penketh South Primary School

THE FLOWER DANCER

Beautiful gardens of flowers surround me,
Blossoming as dusk approaches,
Light dims in the field,
Then a gentle breeze swoops over,
Conducting their dance.

But the breeze gets too rough,
So the flowers don't want to join in,
Therefore the breeze goes away,
Hurt and upset,
The flowers curl up for the night,
With the stars,
Guarding them as they sleep.

Rebecca Keoghan (9)
Penketh South Primary School

BLUE IS ...

Blue is the beautiful sea lying next to the golden sand
Blue is the colour of a tropical bird flying in the air
Blue is the clear sky
Blue is the colour of a pen
Blue is the colour of my eyes

Blue is the wonderful little tropical fish swimming in the sea
Blue is the colour of Brazil's shorts
Blue is the head of a bluebell
Blue is the colour of a blue whale
Blue is the colour of a ruler.

Jack Giblin (9)
Penketh South Primary School

MY LITTLE BROTHER

My little brother is four,
He likes playing with dinosaurs,
He likes playing out on his bike,
My little brother is cute and funny.

My little brother likes going to the zoo,
His favourite animal is a velociraptor,
His favourite food is sausages and beans,
My little brother likes playing on the computer.

My little brother has lots of toys,
He likes eating sweets,
He likes Star Wars action figures,
I love my little brother.

Rebekah Caddick (10)
Penketh South Primary School

VICTORIANS

V is for Vicky in our Christmas play.
I is for ice that people hated so.
C is for children which there were lots of.
T is for treacherous like we think they are.
O is for outside were most people lived.
R is for righteousness which they didn't have.
I is for illness which most people had.
A is for animals that there weren't many of.
N is for nice which they weren't at all.
S is for school which wasn't cool.

Sarah Turner (9)
Penketh South Primary School

RED IS...

Red is a sweet ripe tomato waiting to be picked.
Red is a blazing car light as it is grinding to a halt.
Red is our school jumpers in our classroom.
Red is a wobbly jelly on a plate waiting to be eaten.
Red is a berry on a spiky bramble bush.

Gary Loughead (10)
Penketh South Primary School

BLACK

Black is the misty night sky.
Black is a widow's carefully made funeral dress.
Black is a crow hovering around looking for its dinner.
Black is a witch's cat watching her owner making a potion.
Black is a suit hanging neatly in the wardrobe waiting to be worn.
Black is the fierce stray dog lurking in the dark alley.
Black is a large panther grazing in the sunlight.
Black is the ink from my pen dropping out onto the page
Spelling out words.

Sophie Gilbertson (10)
Penketh South Primary School

RAINBOW

A rainbow is a different coloured banner,
A rainbow is a bunch of different coloured grapes hanging in the sky,
A rainbow is different coloured glitter that falls from the colour fairy,
Was a rainbow bringing colour to our life?

Nicola Warburton (10)
Penketh South Primary School

OPERATION!

'Ouch! My eyes! Ouch!'
I remember when I was four years old,
I'd been thrown down the stairs by my brother,
I had been teasing him all day.

Bang!
I had hit my eye on the radiator,
I was crying my eyes out.
We went to Warrington hospital
And I had my eye checked.

The doctor said if it got worse, come back,
Oh boy, did it get worse.
So the next day we went back
And I had an operation on my eye.

In the operation room I just did not like it,
But in the end it was over pretty quick.
The doctor said it would sting and it did,
So we went home - the next hour.

Daniel McCarthy (10)
Penketh South Primary School

MY DAD

My dad is deep burning red.
He is springtime.
My dad is a gentle, calm breeze.
He's a soft, silky armchair after a hard day at work.
My dad is the wacky Simpsons.
He is a bottle of Coke, full of life.

Jamie Sanderson (11)
St Basil's Catholic Primary School, Widnes

THE WRITER OF THIS POEM
(Based on 'The Writer Of This Poem' by Roger McGough)

As silly as a pup,
As messy as a pig,
As argumentative as a brother in a bath,
As bazaar as a Viking.

As unusual as an alien,
As neat as a housewife,
As noisy as an aeroplane,
As hairy as a gorilla.

As hungry as a pig,
As competitive as a rugby player,
As funny as a clown,
As joyful as Mrs Turner.

As red as a tomato,
As ticklish as a baby,
As annoying as a tap dripping,
As loveable as a kitten.

Natasha Tunstall (10)
St Basil's Catholic Primary School, Widnes

I AM A LITTLE BUMPER CAR

I am a little bumper car, rusty and old,
To my surprise on the windscreen said sold,
I was driven away into a garage with my door hanging off
And my bonnet all bent,
Given new parts and sprayed right down,
But now I'm ready for a ride round town.

Paul Smith (11)
St Basil's Catholic Primary School, Widnes

MY GRANDAD

My grandad is a lovely light-blue.
A scorching summer's day.
He is a winning day at Goodison.
A huge, giant sun, that's been burning through the day.
He is a camouflage waistcoat.
A soft, spongy armchair, after a long day at shooting.
He is Scooby Doo, when he has eaten Scooby snacks all day.
He is a fizzy lager that makes you crazy.

Liam Codd (10)
St Basil's Catholic Primary School, Widnes

MY BEST MATE

He is an icy cold block of white, feather snow.
He is a fun, snow fighting, winter morning.
12:00pm, watching the football in his bedroom.
He is a thundering, winter storm rushing past houses.
He is a dear Nike jumper.
A rock, cold football seat, lumpy and icy.
He is Everton losing against Man U.
A glass of Coke, hyperactive and ready to play football.

Chris McGowan (10)
St Basil's Catholic Primary School, Widnes

MRS TURNER

Mrs Turner is yellow, bright and cheerful.
She is a beautiful, sunny summer.
Mrs Turner is a playground in windy winter.
She is bright and sunny on a hot day.

Mrs Turner is a smart designer suit.
She is a cosy armchair when cuddling her cat.
Mrs Turner is Coronation Street, always having a fuss.
She is a satisfying dinner on a day like today.

Leah Barton (10)
St Basil's Catholic Primary School, Widnes

MY BROTHER

My brother is a bright red Liverpool kit.
He is a joyful, light summer's day.
8:30am at the tennis court.
He is an enormous storm in America,
He is an expensive Lacoste tracky.
He is a smooth table and two hours of football training,
He is the crazy, stressed trick,
He is a Dairy Lea sandwich.

Emily Rowlands (10)
St Basil's Catholic Primary School, Widnes

MR BLUNT

Mr Blunt is as blue as the shirts he wears.
He is the summer sun blazing down on the grass.
He is a 12 o'clock kick-off at Anfield.
A fresh, cool breeze blowing the trees.
He is a tracksuit running round a field.
He is a leather chair watching Liverpool.
Mr Blunt is Coronation Street on a Sunday night.
He is a Mars bar, chewy and tasty.

Chris Buckley (10)
St Basil's Catholic Primary School, Widnes

WONDER HORSE

As I sit on the farmer's fence
Looking, looking at the horse galloping by
Galloping across the field
The wind gently blows his hair
As it stops to rest and graze in the moonlight
It looks up into the starry sky
The moonlight in his eyes
Oh wondering wonder horse

As I sit on the farmer's fence
Wonder horse comes trotting over
As I stroke its sandy white fur
It wanders into the darkness
It wonders what it would be like to be free
And it wishes so hard on a shooting star
That wish might come true
Oh wondering wonder horse

As I sit on the farmer's fence
I get a strange feeling
I sit and wonder
Then I realise what it is
I open the gate, he comes
Off he gallops into the night
Free
Oh wondering wonder horse
I'll be wondering about you.

Suzanna Hughes (11)
St Basil's Catholic Primary School, Widnes

MY CAT

My cat is called Tufty,
He's really dumb and dazy.
He goes to sleep, then watches traffic,
Tufty is so lazy.

Every time he closes his eyes,
The next minute he is snoring.
He miaows at us 24-7
But doesn't come when we're calling.

Tufty is a monster with food,
He rips your hand off too.
If you hold out something for him to eat,
You can hear his sloppy chew.

He's always playing with us,
And fighting with us too.
He sits on the stairs and sometimes falls off,
His balance, he never knew.

Tufty is so cute though,
On the outside I mean.
When you shout at him he makes you feel so guilty,
But it's him though it seems!

To sum up Tufty,
I would have to say,
The most perfect cat
For every day!

Lucy-May Amos Roscoe (11)
St Basil's Catholic Primary School, Widnes

FLIGHT

Grind, grind of the engine,
Whoosh, whoosh, of the propeller,
Speeding down the runway,
Up, up and away!

Climbing cautiously to space
Plummeting through the fluffy white clouds,
Loop-the-loop, swooping upside down,
The rattling of the engine stops.

Silence!
The plane plunges down,
As soon as it nearly hits the ground,
Rattle! Rattle! The engine starts.

Puff, a cloud of acrid water comes from the plane
Gliding on silent wings,
Landing with a bump,
The wind of the propeller slowing down,
That is the end of the stunt!

Daniel Seager (11)
St John the Evangelist CE Aided Primary School, Macclesfield

THE DEPTHS

Sinking deeper and deeper,
Losing more and more breath,
I see the crabs as silent creepers
Will I come face to face with death?

Past me the coral is glistening,
Pearls bubble by my side.
It's almost as if the fishes are listening,
To my thoughts in the murkiness far and wide.

I'm drowning more and more,
And the darkness is merging around me,
The sharks plunge to the ocean floor,
Down in the depths of the sea.

Jessica Taylor (11)
St John the Evangelist CE Aided Primary School, Macclesfield

THE DEPTHS

In the depths of my tummy
I've eaten a meal which was scrummy,
there was a main course,
smothered in sweet tomato sauce.

A lovely chocolate biscuit,
you never know it might be from the Lake District.
At the bottom of my tummy,
lies a red spicy chilli.

On the third shelf of my stomach,
lurks a bunch of soggy chips,
dipped in Mexican spicy dips,
which give me bad stomach ache.

A bubbling soup is gurgling loud
as I looked through the starters, then it was found.
Brown bread buttered,
malt loaf, syrup covered.

Dessert, hot fudge in chocolate is dipped,
some lemon meringue, in cream it's whipped.
The taste of hot sticky pudding,
makes my eyes with water flooding.

Jodie Burgess (10)
St John the Evangelist CE Aided Primary School, Macclesfield

FLIGHT

High in the sky
Like a bird I fly.
I ride on silent wings
Below the bell tower rings.

Below I can see
Eyes watching me,
The wind whistling
My beak glistening.

I fly with the flock
Over the dock,
Feathery are my wings,
My fellow friend sings.

Southward we fly,
High in the sky,
The sun sinks low
In a golden glow.

What mysteries lie below?
Before long the wind will blow,
My whole family is
Flying south with me.

Matthew Taylor (10)
St John the Evangelist CE Aided Primary School, Macclesfield

MY DOG

My dog can play football,
He's like Elvis too,
His hair is black,
And he wears dark glasses!

My brother and I,
Like playing with him,
To give him a treat,
He has biscuits for tea.

Jack Rawlins (9)
St John the Evangelist CE Aided Primary School, Macclesfield

FLIGHT

Looking up at the other birds fly,
Swooping, diving in the sky,
Soaring up higher than high,
Why can't I?
Why can't I fly?

They have no problem flying,
They don't need to think about trying
To glide, to fly,
Why can't I?
Why can't I fly?

Looking at them plunging down,
Ruffling my feathers as I frown,
The whistling wind flies past my beak,
Why can't I?
Why can't I fly?

They plummet past my sulking face,
Whooshing down with elegant grace,
Some collide but most fly,
Oh why? Oh why?
Why can't I fly?

Jennifer Bucknell (11)
St John the Evangelist CE Aided Primary School, Macclesfield

THE DEPTHS

Coral glistens as I swim past,
While fish dive under a shipwreck's mast.
Valuable pearls that oysters hold,
Which divers will find, soon to be sold.
Filtered sunshine seeps through the water,
My oxygen level slowly growing shorter.
Secrets are hidden amongst the creatures,
One of the ocean's most mystical features.

Silence lives there without a sound,
But somewhere there's a noise waiting to be found.
I glide on into the unknown world,
Where fish are flat and seaweed is curled.
Delicate plants lie ignored in the caves,
Merely missing the cool blue waves.
Beautiful colours dazzle my eyes,
Colours of fish of every different size.

Carnivorous crabs hide around the stones,
Living secretly in their undercover homes.
Sharks scan for creatures lying on the sand,
If one saw me it could take off my hand.
Now I realise I've reached my goal,
To swim underwater and join in with a shoal.
I don't want to leave this wonderful place,
So back I go at a very slow pace.

Corinne Pinder (10)
St John the Evangelist CE Aided Primary School, Macclesfield

THE STAR I SAW IN THE SKY

I gazed at the star in the sky.
It winked at me, then waved goodbye.
I found that strange, we all know why
That talking star, in the sky.

'Oh bright shining star, up in the sky
Why do you talk so much?'
He said, 'Simple,' and I asked why
'Because I'm a star in the sky,'
                    . . . he said!

Imogen Ault (9)
St John the Evangelist CE Aided Primary School, Macclesfield

FLIGHT

Drfiting along in a fluffy cloud,
The wind was whistling very loud.
She dreamt this dream once again,
Flying out of a windowpane.

Up, up and away she went,
Wings that were given, not lent,
Gliding down and flying high,
Soaring up into the sky.

She landed now on top of a tree,
She picked berries and went to see
A plane soaring in the sky,
She was glad that she could fly.

The wind was moaning in her ear,
The scent of air filled her nose
Touching clouds with no fear
She plummeted down and then froze.

She walked into her bedroom
And then she slept
She was glad that she had kept her wings
Which did not bring her doom
Now that she was in her room.

Emma Stell (10)
St John the Evangelist CE Aided Primary School, Macclesfield

A Poem To Be Spoken Loudly

It was so noisy that I heard
drums banging
in a colourful festival parade . . .

It was so deafening that I heard
an elephant
stamping around in a busy zoo . . .

It was so explosive that I heard
fireworks exploding
in the smoky night sky . . .

It was so blustery that I felt the
wind cutting
through my skin outside the front door . . .

It was so shrilling that I heard
shouting children
running across the gloomy playground.

Elizabeth Moss (8)
St John the Evangelist CE Aided Primary School, Macclesfield

My Brother

I have a little brother,
Jordan is his name.
Whenever he is naughty,
I always get the blame.

He comes into my bedroom,
He messes up my toys.
He scribbles in my books,
I'm not sure that I like boys.

He's always up to mischief,
When Mummy's not around.
He's always very noisy
And I don't make a sound.

Dad said, 'I think we'll sell him,
And buy a dog instead.'
But I love my little brother
He's the best thing since sliced bread.

Sophie Frith (7)
St John the Evangelist CE Aided Primary School, Macclesfield

THE EVIL MUCUS MUTANT VIPER

The evil mucus mutant viper's crawling up your nose,
It's oozing through your windpipe,
Now it's crawling out your toes,
If you use a microscope,
You are sure to see,
The tiny little barb-like sting that'll kill you before tea!

It's taken over your body
And now you're turning green
And you're now becoming thin
You're a sludgy runner bean!
Your eyes are on green sticks
And they represent a pin!

The evil mucus mutant viper's eating up your brains.
Now he's being stupid and he's doing it again.
Oh look, he's in a swimming pool
Of blood and guts and gore,
Your hands are shrinking slowly
And your eyes are getting sore!

Andrew Pickles (9)
St John the Evangelist CE Aided Primary School, Macclesfield

FLANDERS FIELD

Waiting here until the night
To be seen,
Or maybe not.
Wishing for this thing to stop.

Dreadful things to the eye,
And the inside ear.
Blood, bullets, watching explosions.
Sounding guns and screaming soldiers.

Carried from the field
Maybe alive or maybe dead.
Slumped on shoulders
Until in the trench.

Now I hear people say,
'Is he alive or is he dead?'
Some say dead, some say alive.
Now they know, since here
I am lying in a hospital bed.

Charlotte Hyde (9)
St John the Evangelist CE Aided Primary School, Macclesfield

THE DEPTHS

Down, down, down I go,
Down to the deep blue jewel below,
Fishes swimming, barging past,
Sharks racing, diving fast.

Precious jewels in a box they lay,
I'll pick them up and take them away,
Coral on the ground glistened,
Silent sea creatures stopped and listened.

Seaweed swayed from side to side,
Frightened jellyfish stopped to hide,
What mysteries lie below
Like the angelfish that's extremely slow?

My air tank's running out of air,
I've not been down here long, this isn't fair,
I might never come down here again, no never,
I want to stay here forever and ever.

Sarah Sharpley (11)
St John the Evangelist CE Aided Primary School, Macclesfield

THE DEPTHS

The depths of the gloomy graveyard
The groans of the mumbling graves
Secrets hidden in a block of stone
Nothing remains, no flesh, just bones

Sorrowing sighs heard from around
All in the beat of a heart pound
People surrounded with a shivering spine
They thought they saw Frankenstein

Every face was as pale as the moon
And then I heard a striking *boom!*
People ran into their house
But I stayed, as quiet as a mouse.

The rain poured from the sky
All in a instant, a blink of a eye
This experience made me see light
The depths of the graveyard that fearful night!

Cody Ives-Keeler (11)
St John the Evangelist CE Aided Primary School, Macclesfield

SWIM WITH ME TO MY TROPICAL ISLAND

Swim with me to my paradise island
Swim in my luxury lagoon
You can pick my mangoes
And ride my elephants.

See my dancing flamingos
And see my twirling starfish
Come swim with me for a heavenly island
Look at my paradise birds.

A passion for pineapple
A tangy taste
And a tasty mango drink
Whilst scorching sun beats down on your back
Swim with me - quick, pack!
Banana trees with big juicy leaves
Passion flowers -
You can stay for hours
Swim with me to my paradise island.

Naomi Thomas
St John the Evangelist CE Aided Primary School, Macclesfield

A POEM TO BE SPOKEN LOUDLY

It was so deafening that I felt
an earthquake crashing through the earth's crust
Splitting through the ground like a jigsaw.

It was so noisy that I heard
drums banging like thunder
crashing in the sky.

It was so booming that I heard
an elephant strolling through a wild forest
making dirty footprints on the stony ground.

It was so ear-splitting that I heard
fireworks shooting into the sky
making patterns of decoration.

Simone Longden (9)
St John the Evangelist CE Aided Primary School, Macclesfield

FLIGHT

Away from the world my flapping wings take me,
High up close to the heavens I float,
Then I spot a vole scampering over the meadow,
Fast I plummet and catch it in my welcoming beak.
When the moon rises and the humans fall asleep,
I fly over cars,
I fly to the stars,
But most of all I want to fly to the moon.

Floating on silent wings I think
Being a bird is just like a dream,
As a bird you can fly and fly to the heavens above,
You can fly over oceans and rivers,
Being able to fly is just so wonderful
Flight is so wonderful
I love to feel the breeze ruffle my feathers,
In the freedom of the skies.

Rosie Barker (10)
St John the Evangelist CE Aided Primary School, Macclesfield

FLIGHT

It was the flight of the kite
In the sunlight.
It swooped in the air
everywhere.

It sparkled with colours
red, blue and green.
I pulled on the strings
and made it go high,
high in the sky.

It waved in the sun
and my dad said, 'Well done.'
The wind pushed and pulled
whistled and blew.
It flew like a plane
straight down the lane
and back again.

The crowd laughed and clapped
Screamed and yelled
blew and whistled.
The kite was floating
changing colours
flying in slow motion.

The kite came down
time to rest
I had done my very best.
It came down slowly
Swooping and looping
then it landed
on the soft green grass.

Abbey Dowse (10)
St John the Evangelist CE Aided Primary School, Macclesfield

THE DEPTHS

In the depths of my tummy,
Lurks something yummy,
Like chocolate chip cookies
And lemon-flavoured lollies,
Strawberry-jammed toast,
And McDonald's French fries which I love the most.

Also some vanilla ice cream,
And vegetables which are mean.
A nice Saturday pork chop
And a Sunday night lamb chop
A lovely digestive biscuit
Maybe it came from the Lake District,
A Willy Wonka's exploder,
And, fruit roller.

Living at the bottom of my tummy,
Is a spicy chicken curry.
A lovely tinfoiled turkey
And marshmallows very jerky.
A piece of crispy bacon
And a milkshake stirred, not shaken.
The other day I tried a soufflé
It wasn't great but it was okay.
A lovely chicken drummer,
And some water which I drink in summer.
Some chocolate mousse
And pure orange juice.
A piece of beautiful salmon
And an extra big gammon.

What I love to eat - scrambled eggs
But what I hate - horrible frogs' legs.

Ashleigh Hehir (10)
St John the Evangelist CE Aided Primary School, Macclesfield

PUPPIES OR KITTENS

Puppies are cute, kittens are cuddly,
But when I can't decide, I get muddly,
Puppies or kittens, I can't decide,
They're all so cute, I don't really mind.

What could I call it? What to do?
Should I let it play in my shoe?
Should it be a girl or boy?
Should I buy it a brand new toy?

Kittens play with balls of wool,
Give them one, they will give it a pull,
They also chase lights on walls,
Mistaking them for woolly balls!

Puppies like to fetch sticks,
They also like to knock down bricks!
Chasing tails is a favourite too,
Slippers perfect for a chew.

If I get a dog or cat,
Its name will be Matt,
But if it is a cute girl,
Its name will definitely be Pearl.

Puppies or kittens? I still can't decide,
They are all so cute and also so kind,
Their cute faces are sweet like honey,
Although they cost a lot of money.

Puppies or kittens,
I still can't decide,
I know what to do!
I'll have two.

Gemma Brown (10)
St John the Evangelist CE Aided Primary School, Macclesfield

THE ZOO

We're off to the zoo
Yippitee-do
We're off to the zoo
Me and you

We're off to the zoo
Driving in the car
We're off to the zoo
It can't be far

We're off to the zoo
We can't be late
We're here at the zoo
And we've arrived at the gate

We're here at the zoo
We enter the gate
We're here at the zoo
All the animals are great.

The chimpanzees swing
While parrots sing
We see the seals being fed
And lazy lions sleep in a straw bed

Dolphins dive through their pool
And tigers try to keep themselves cool
Monkeys swing from tree to tree
We're so exhausted, you and me.

As we get back into the car
We set off home, it isn't far
As we travel all the way home
We leave the animals all on their own.

Elanah Grace Foster (8)
St John the Evangelist CE Aided Primary School, Macclesfield

FLIGHT

Sky diving high in the sky
Seeing people as tiny specks,
Watching birds soaring down,
Whistling wind howls in my ear
Cutting through the air
As though it was tissue paper.

I think for a moment I have wings,
Floating down, down to the ground
Plummeting like an eagle catching its prey.
Gliding gracefully down to the sea-like sky
Shortened time as I float down to Earth
Sharp short pains on my body as the wind
                            is catching my clothes.

One strong tug at the rope
And up, up, up, my parachute goes
Making me fly back into its wing
Slowly I drop, gliding I go
Waiting till I stop on the ground
Waiting, waiting, waiting.

Slowly I drop to the ground,
Thinking of the great experience I've had
Dropping from the plane and gliding
Floating down to the ground.
Stopping like a caterpillar curling up
Landing on the lush grass.

I had the freedom of the skies
I could do whatever I wanted
Rolling around doing handstands
Rolling over without any care at all.
The great sensation filled my mind.

Victoria Hordern (10)
St John the Evangelist CE Aided Primary School, Macclesfield

THE DEPTHS

Grab your ticket, entry to the
London Underground,
Let's go for a ride,
Brace yourselves,
By my side.
Hop on the train
Don't be shy
This is the lane
It will be fun, and that's not a lie.
Whoosh! Goes the door
As it closes shut
This is a fast train
That's why I chose this
Down to Bond Street
Then King's Cross
Take a seat,
That's right, Ross
Then we start moving
Clacketty-clack
Through the tunnel
Watch your back
Faster! Faster!
As we go
Don't be scared
I'm not a foe
Start to slow down
As we reach the station
We're a bit late
What devastation!
Open the door
Wake up from your nap
All we say now is
Mind the gap!

Oliver Gould (10)
St John the Evangelist CE Aided Primary School, Macclesfield

FLIGHT

Here I am in a hot air balloon
At 3 o'clock in the afternoon
It's huge and big
Like a really big pig
And as you travel through the air
The wind will push and swish your hair.

The balloon is moving very slowly
But I'm still in one piece and holy
But now it's getting fast and quicker
As it does, I am getting sicker
Now I look up into the sky
It's blue and bright and very high.

As I reach my hands out far
I almost touch a wishing star
But all the air feels clean and fresher
It's like you're going over Cheshire.

In the air you taste just nothing
It only tastes like lumps of stuffing
It's not very nice sticking your tongue out anyway
But I won't do it any day.

As I'm high I see a great big herd
And even flying by is a bird
I see a lot of colours here
There's blue for the sky and brown for a deer
It's getting darker, out comes the moon
So that's my day in a hot air balloon.

Leanne Melling (11)
St John the Evangelist CE Aided Primary School, Macclesfield

THE WITCHES' SPELL

Frogs and toads
Maggots and rabbits
Eye of newt.
Stir! Stir!
Bubble and boil.

Hocus pocus diddly-doo
Canasea Darry look at you.
If you dare to come
I will have your thumb.

Heads and legs
Weeds and seeds
Black cat's whisker
Stir! Stir!
Bubble and boil
Hocus pocus diddly-doo
Canasea Darry look at you
If you dare to come
I will have your bum.

Toes and nose
Claws and jaws
Lips of camel
Stir! Stir!
Bubble and boil
Hocus pocus diddly-doo
Canasea Darry look at you
If you dare to come
I will have your *tum!*

Rachel Ann Knight (9)
St John the Evangelist CE Aided Primary School, Macclesfield

FLIGHT

As I glide through the sky,
the misty clouds meet my side,
hills ahead, sheep down below,
find me somewhere else to go.

Greeny grass, leafy trees,
gladly-playing children freeze,
the misty moon starts weaning off,
oh guess what? I've seen a moth.

Stars are out, getting late,
shiny stars are shining light,
getting tired, must rest now,
see you in the morning,
I'll take you out.

As I'm coming in to land,
a day from a glider has come to an end.

Danielle L Hallworth (10)
St John the Evangelist CE Aided Primary School, Macclesfield

INUIT CHANT

There is a panic in feeling
the cold strength of the blizzard.

Come to the great world
and see small creatures
going down into the earth
in the winter months.

Jordan Riley (7)
St John the Evangelist CE Aided Primary School, Macclesfield

FLIGHT

A proud bird stands
Covered in mechanics
Rusting and rotting away
Turn of key, puff of smoke
And there lies a ray of hope.
Under the rusty dust, a bluebird rests.
Mechanically rekindling a long-lost machine
Spanners tighten nuts and bolts
Welders weld bits of metal
Mechanics shout, 'She's gone.'
A click of the engine
A puff of smoke
That was when we lost all hope!

Stuart G Whittaker (10)
St John the Evangelist CE Aided Primary School, Macclesfield

FLIGHT

10, 9, 8, 7, 6, 5, 4, 3, 2, 1, we have lift-off,
The engines *roared!*
As the rocket shot up into the blue sky.
Apollo Z shot up into the dark sky
Like a bullet from a gun.

Its destination, the planets where no man had been before.

The stars shone brightly, you could see
Orion, Scorpio and Cancer.
Square planets, spinning planets and others.
'You have arrived at your destination.'

Stefan Carney (10)
St John the Evangelist CE Aided Primary School, Macclesfield

A Poem To Be Spoken Loudly

It was so loud that I heard
the currents blasting the sea to spray
like white breathing horses gliding
in the ocean.

It was so rowdy that I heard
A huge terrorising volcano full of red hot lava
shooting out of its rock.

It was so deafening that I heard
rumbling fireworks blasting into a huge spiky
flash of colours in the air.

It was so loud that I felt
an earthquake shaking the solid earth.

Calum Robertson (8)
St John the Evangelist CE Aided Primary School, Macclesfield

Flight

Taking flight, off we go
My wings are armed with dangerous ammo.
Into combat, here I go!

My body is silver and my wings also
My engines are grey though.
They are powerful, they're what make me go.

As I look down at the world below,
The houses are pinpricks
And the cars are moving matches on the road.

Sam Lowe (10)
St John the Evangelist CE Aided Primary School, Macclesfield

ALL THE ANIMALS THAT I'VE SEEN

I saw a cat that sat on a mat.
I saw a dog in the fog.
I saw a fox in a box.
I saw a pig wearing a wig.
I saw a mouse in our house.
I saw a fish on my dish.
I saw a bear brushing his hair.
I saw a snake by a lake.
I saw a frog that sat on a log.
I saw a fly up in the sky.
I saw a sheep that did a leap.
I saw a whale that had a very large tail.
All the animals that I've seen have often
                      been in my dreams!

Chloe Furness (8)
St John the Evangelist CE Aided Primary School, Macclesfield

FLIGHT

High in the sky,
I'm trying to fly,
Wind whistling in my ear,
It hurts me so much I feel a tear.

Up, up and away,
I could fly all day,
Cutting through the air,
The clouds like fluffy polar bears.

As I look down from high above
I feel like a gentle, peace-bringing dove.

Chris Holland (10)
St John the Evangelist CE Aided Primary School, Macclesfield

THE DEPTHS

Deep in the depths of the silent blue sea,
Coral is glistening as bright as can be.

Fishes swim beneath the seaweed,
Green as grass, light as a feather.

In the murky depths of the ocean
Lies a shipwreck abandoned - below.

Lost in the blue depths
Is a treasure chest unopened.

A mysterious cave dark and dingy,
Where bubbles leak from the entrance.

Crabs scuttle quickly through the sand.
Past glistening pearls upon the rocks.

Jellyfish floating in the water with a fluorescent glow,
Deep in the murky depths below.

Sophie Avery (11)
St John the Evangelist CE Aided Primary School, Macclesfield

WAR

War is red
It smells of hot gunpowder
War tastes like blood
It sounds like fireworks
It feels cold
War lives in the heart of a battlefield!

Joshua Thomas (9)
St John the Evangelist CE Aided Primary School, Macclesfield

THE DEPTHS

Giant tigers roam the land.
Slithery snakes twist round the bendy branches of the tall treetops.
Huge, hairy lions pounce on tarantulas, twice the size of your fist.
Curled-up cockroaches sleeping under leafy canopies.

Tiny beetles scuttling along the jungle floor.
Unheard of centipedes spiralling on rocks.
Squawking parrots sitting on treetops away from danger.
Inquisitive monkeys swinging from branch to branch.

Shaking trees as gorillas clamber up them.
Wiggling worms under grey round rocks.
Huge wings fluttering past the other animals of the jungle.
Minute ants getting squashed every second.

I would love to live in this fantastic place!

Claire Taylor (10)
St John the Evangelist CE Aided Primary School, Macclesfield

COLOURS

Pink, purple, yellow and blue
Do you like these colours?
Well I do . . .

Silver, gold, bronze and red,
See all the colours
In your head . . .

Orange, turquoise, aqua and green
All beautiful colours
The best you have ever seen.

Melanie Knight (9)
St John the Evangelist CE Aided Primary School, Macclesfield

THE EAGLE

He leaves the side of his wife and child,
Flying out into the wild.
His talons, sharp and shiny,
The great power, God Almighty,
His crown on the flag of Liberty,
Flying in life for eternity.
Suddenly he sees his prey,
Plunging down in a flash of grey,
He screams, his cry of strength,
Stretching his wings at full length.
His great claws crush the prey,
What a great hunt today.
He soars back into the sky,
Now he's just out to fly.
Holding to it with dear life,
He has to get it back to his wife.
He returns to the side of his mate and child,
Returning back from the wild.

Jordan Kenyon (11)
St John the Evangelist CE Aided Primary School, Macclesfield

MY CHANT

There is a rough wind
Feel the breeze go up your fingertips.
Come to the great world
and see the trees sway to and fro.
Follow its whistling sound
In the early dawn.

Leah Gleaves (8)
St John the Evangelist CE Aided Primary School, Macclesfield

A POEM TO BE SPOKEN LOUDLY

It was so noisy that I heard
people screaming on a roller coaster
as it tipped upside down.

It was so breathtaking that I heard
dolphins gliding in the oceans,
splashing the waves.

It was so deafening that I heard
banging fireworks booming up in the smoky air
making beautiful decorations.

It was so loud that I heard
drums banging like an elephant
stomping on the ground.

Eleanor Thomason (8)
St John the Evangelist CE Aided Primary School, Macclesfield

A POEM TO BE SPOKEN LOUDLY

It was so rowdy that I heard
Wind crashing against the windowpane.

It was so deafening that I heard
Monstrous cars shake Earth's rattling floor
Outside on the midnight road.

It was so blaring that I heard
A mysterious black cat scratch a piece of squeaky metal.

It was so shrill that I felt
Music vibrating through my tiny body.

Robert Phythian (9)
St John the Evangelist CE Aided Primary School, Macclesfield

A POEM TO BE SPOKEN LOUDLY

It was so noisy that I heard
blustery winds howling,
rocking through petrified trees . . .

It was so blaring that I heard
volcanoes erupting, spitting
out fiery lava onto a scared town.

It was so deafening that I heard . . .
sea crashing against the boulders
of a rocky cliff.

It was so noisy that I felt . . .
rumbling earthquakes knocking
buildings to the ground.

It was so shrilling that I heard . . .
fireworks whizzing
up to the gloomy dark sky.

Alistair Williamson (8)
St John the Evangelist CE Aided Primary School, Macclesfield

PAIN

Pain is like fading grey
It smells like burnt, rotten bodies
It tastes like bubbling blood
Pain is like a sharp knife through your heart
It feels like a muscle being ripped apart
It lies in a graveyard.

James Moss (9)
St John the Evangelist CE Aided Primary School, Macclesfield

ONE POWERFUL POEM

It was so noisy that I heard
aeroplanes' engines shooting
through the stormy clouds . . .

It was so deafening that I heard
elephants rattling
their cages at the zoo . . .

It was so shrilling that I heard
an owl hooting
in the cold night . . .

It was so loud that I felt
the Earth shivering
in the misty early morning . . .

It was so booming that I heard
a motorbike crashing
on slippery ice . . .

Abigail Walker (9)
St John the Evangelist CE Aided Primary School, Macclesfield

DEATH

    Death is red and gloomy
It smells like rotten bones in a cave.
    Death tastes like burning blood.
It sounds like wolves howling.
    Death feels like sadness and pain.
Death lives in the heart of a dragon.

Rachel Barber (9)
St John the Evangelist CE Aided Primary School, Macclesfield

A POWERFUL POEM TO BE SPOKEN LOUDLY

It was so noisy that I heard
an aeroplane engine screaming
through the stormy clouds . . .

It was so deafening that I heard
at the friendly zoo
an elephant rattling its cage . . .

It was so shrilling that I felt
in the early morning
the earth shaking in early mist . . .

It was so loud that I heard
an owl hooting
in the midnight mist.

Hannah Davis (8)
St John the Evangelist CE Aided Primary School, Macclesfield

IN THE FIELDS OF THE DEAD

In the fields of the dead,
People who were once alive are dead,
Friends who were alive are now dead,
In the fields of the dead.

In the fields of the dead,
Where battles once took place,
Brave men died for their country,
Courageous men died for their country,
In the fields of the dead.

Duncan Littlechild (9)
St John the Evangelist CE Aided Primary School, Macclesfield

A Poem To Be Spoken Loudly

It was so booming that I heard
a demolition ring clanking
against tattered flats

It was so deafening that I heard
sandy rock blocks falling
from the gigantic pyramid

It was so ear-splitting that I heard
the scraping of a bearded man carving
a stone grave at the silent church

It was so noisy that I felt
the stampede of angry elephants
across the wide world in boiling Africa

It was so rowdy that I heard
the piercing splinters fly out
as the petrified car crashed off the road
into the wooden fence.

Charlotte Hobbs (9)
St John the Evangelist CE Aided Primary School, Macclesfield

Inuit Chant

There is a danger in
Feeling the coldness
Come to the great world
And see the skating ice
Over the Earth.
Follow the polar bears
In the cold winter.

Laura Baggs (7)
St John the Evangelist CE Aided Primary School, Macclesfield

NOISES

It was so noisy that I heard . . .
howling winds knocking down
petrified trees.

It was so blaring that I heard . . .
an erupting volcano spitting out
fiery lava onto the town.

It was so deafening that I heard . . .
sea crashing
on the boulders of rock-hard cliffs.

It was so boisterous that I felt . . .
a rumbling earthquake shaking
below my feet.

Joel Frost (8)
St John the Evangelist CE Aided Primary School, Macclesfield

MY PUPPY

My puppy is sweet
and loves to eat.
My puppy likes to play about
on the soft green grass,

And smell the pollen on silky flowers.
My puppy loves to chew on a juicy bone
or lick a big ice cream cone.

My puppy loves to play with her ball
day or night and snores so loud
it gives you a fright.

Eloise Cantwell (7)
St John the Evangelist CE Aided Primary School, Macclesfield

ONE POWERFUL POEM

It was so noisy that I heard
fireworks exploding
in the misty sky . . .

It was so boisterous that I heard
aeroplanes rumbling
in the night air . . .

It was so booming that I heard
rockets shooting
in the air . . .

It was so noisy that I heard
machines twisting around
making clanking noises . . .

Jack Johnson (8)
St John the Evangelist CE Aided Primary School, Macclesfield

FLANDERS FIELD

In Flanders field bodies lie,
Rifle shells fly.
Screams from soldiers being shot,
RAF biplanes fly by.

In Flanders field skylarks fly,
We eat our rations,
We start chatting when our friends die.
We stagger across the muddy fields.
In Flanders field our bodies lie.

Ian Prior (9)
St John the Evangelist CE Aided Primary School, Macclesfield

A Noisy Poem To Be Spoken Loudly

It was so noisy that I heard
fireworks shooting
up into the smoky night air
like decorations.

People shouting
and disturbing the silence.
Windows breaking
and falling through the air
like sparkling decorations.

It was so shrilling that I felt
the sea crash on grey rocks.

It was so blaring that I heard
drums beating in a band
outside my house.

Christopher Littlechild (8)
St John the Evangelist CE Aided Primary School, Macclesfield

Beauty

Beauty is a sweet light violet,
It smells like newly-grown roses.
Beauty tastes like a juicy ripe peach,
It sounds like the song of a bird.
Beauty feels like soft velvet petals,
It lives in peaceful Heaven.

Bethany Holt (9)
St John the Evangelist CE Aided Primary School, Macclesfield

THE BIRD OF PARADISE

Its spectacular wings cover its face
It glides down with elegant grace
Swooping down through sunlit trees,
A dart of blue, but nobody sees,
The bird of paradise.

A splash of red, silky and bright,
Shines beautifully in the light.
His feathers laid flat, soft and sleek,
His bright eyes and pointy beak,
The bird of paradise.

Sitting in its cosy nest,
Far more stunning than the rest.
He flies away through the sky,
Like a gentle butterfly,
The bird of paradise.

Katie Bucknell (8)
St John the Evangelist CE Aided Primary School, Macclesfield

PAIN

Pain is the colour of rotten bones
It smells like rotten tomatoes
It tastes like bitter blood
Pain sounds like a body screaming
It feels like agony
It lives in the ground.

Sam Edwards (9)
St John the Evangelist CE Aided Primary School, Macclesfield

MY CAT

My cat is called Puffy,
He is also fluffy,
And he drinks milk,
And feels like silk.

My cat never forgets his toys,
Only he plays with girls and boys,
He eats fish,
On a dish.

My cat is in bed,
And he sleeps in a shed,
He is snuggling in his basket,
Made out of elastic.

Nicola Pheasey (8)
St John the Evangelist CE Aided Primary School, Macclesfield

WINDY NIGHTS

Whenever the man came out at night
Whenever the tree began to whine
A galloping horse covered in white
I wish you could turn back the time
All of the fires have been put out
Why does he gallop and gallop about?

Whenever the moon and stars are set
Whenever the grass is damp and wet
Riding his white horse that is his pet
He murders the people that come and go
He always grabs the people he knows
Why does he dress up in black and white?

Jordan Bettany (9)
St John the Evangelist CE Aided Primary School, Macclesfield

MY PET POLAR BEAR

My pet polar bear is soft and round
He weighs less than 500 pounds
His nose is slimy and very wet
He doesn't go fishing with a fishing net.

My pet polar bear lives in the sea
He doesn't open his house with a key
To cook his food he doesn't use gas
He trades the fish that he has.

My pet polar bear loves to swim
Even though the sky is dim
He will play with seals
He hates all eels.

That's what my pet polar bear likes to do.

Hannah Errington (8)
St John the Evangelist CE Aided Primary School, Macclesfield

MY OWN SECRET ISLAND

I wish I had my own secret island
With lots of coconuts
Millions of flowers
And special little huts.

No adults to shout
Or big sisters to boss you about
I'd make a coconut shell drink every day
And I really think that the best place in the world
                             is my own *secret island.*

Georgina Whitworth (8)
St John the Evangelist CE Aided Primary School, Macclesfield

BUT THE CAT SAT STILL

The kitten played cheerfully
The zebras munched slowly
The lamb ran hyperactively
The cow grazed peacefully
But the cat sat still.

The giraffe licked happily
The pig ate greedily
The snake slithered swiftly
The chick chirped excitedly
But the cat sat still.

The chicken flapped madly
The dolphin leaped acrobatically
The jaguar pounced unexpectedly
The frog jumped suddenly
But the cat sat still.

Elisha Bradley (8)
St John the Evangelist CE Aided Primary School, Macclesfield

PAIN

Pain is crimson.
It smells like a dead pig.
Pain tastes like a banana.
It sounds like a dreaded human.
It feels like ice.
Pain lives in you.

Chris Graves (9)
St John the Evangelist CE Aided Primary School, Macclesfield

COME ON INTO MY LUSCIOUS GARDEN

Come on into my luscious garden
Come in and have a laugh.
Taste my fruit cake and my juicy pine drink
Come on in, please come on in.

Yes, you can stand on my bouncy hammock
And feel the fragrant breeze out in my palm trees
You can pick my hibiscus
And kiss my chimpanzees.

You can jump up in the grass
And if you pick up a flea
I'll take you down for a quick dip in the sea.
Believe me, there's nothing better than
Coming into my luscious garden.

Sam Avery (8)
St John the Evangelist CE Aided Primary School, Macclesfield

THE OWL

Ever watchful the speckled tawny owl perches on his
bridge-like branch like an heir to the throne.
His piercing beak drives into a meadow mouse.
His hazel feathers ruffle as the wind passes through him.
His eyes are coal staring into the eerie night.
His wings like a flag flapping in the wind.
His grappling hook claws cling onto mice, branches and voles.
He is master of the wood.

Gabriel Derbyshire (10)
St Mary's CE Primary School, Sale

CONFLAGRATION

C atapulting fireballs collapse from towering pillars trapping desperate children fighting through the flames for their merciful lives.
O blivious, grotesque shapes emerge from the pit of calling fire.
N on-stop, never-ending, continuing through the day.
F ighting flames, destroying helpless people's lives.
L ate night falls, a shadow of horror creeping over like a monster of doom.
A nguish spreads a blanket of fear, fear for their families, their home and their lives.
G ruesome fights, the city ablaze, the city's defeat.
R elentless, rampaging rage, the heart of the fire.
A ching heads, aching hearts. Is there to be an end?
T errifying smoke chokes the conurbation.
I llusion, smoke playing with minds.
O beying the city's desperate plea, the master of destruction, gone - leaving only shattered hearts and homes.
N ever again will they see their belongings, for their belongings and loved ones are now being digested in the fire's belly, taking everything, leaving nothing.

Laura Anderson (10)
St Mary's CE Primary School, Sale

PRINCE OF THE SILENT AIR

He glides elegantly, listening, listening. His snowy white feathers are the beauty of the night, whilst obedient trees offer places to land. His wise eyes are powerful telescopes whilst alert ears are ever listening, listening.

Suddenly a rustling is heard far below, the prince spreads his magnificent ivory wings and dives. A miniature dormouse scrambles, not knowing of the oncoming dread.

A horror-struck mouse, transfixed - as sinister claws grip
firmly around the petite body, scarcely trembling.
Fighting desperately, the tired mouse capitulates to the menacing
prince still listening, listening for another unfortunate dormouse.
The terrified dormouse remembers his famished, frightened family.
Will he survive?

The skilful hunter returns to his owlets, congratulating himself
on his catch. Still listening, listening.

Alexander Law (11)
St Mary's CE Primary School, Sale

PRINCE OF THE SILENT AIR

The prince of the silent air, sits proudly on a gnarled branch
ready to swoop down daringly, like a cart falling off the edge
of a roller coaster. Scrutinising the dark foliage, the wide owl
distends his dappled wings, his eyes transfixed on the
unsuspecting prey.

The terror stricken mouse runs whilst thinking of his
famished family. The wise owl clasped into the intimidated mouse
like a brake on a car. Swooping through the ebony night, the
petrified mouse tries to break free from the piercing claws.

Coming to a halt, the prince of the silent air, descends
the transfixed mouse into his cluttered nest.
The mouse is a stone statue.

Alexandra Cambridge (10)
St Mary's CE Primary School, Sale

My Brother

I have a little brother
Whom I really hate
He's great at being annoying
And he gets me in a state.

He's always taking my stuff
And being really bad
Why is he my brother,
He's acting like my dad?

I'm always in lots of trouble
Why? It's because of him!
He's very, very evil
I want to throw him in a bin.

He's always on the PlayStation
Oh, it's not fair
He's really, really smelly
In his underwear

One day I will get him
I really, really will
I guess I'm only joking though,
My brother's really brill!

Sarah Potter (10)
The Dale Primary School

My Room

My room is dark and dingy and creepy in the night.
The noises give me quite a fright,
It seems someone's watching me, though the curtains are closed.
Is it just my mind or is there someone out there?
If there is . . . who?

Chris Barker (10)
The Dale Primary School

DARK

I used to have a fear of the dark,
A three year old girl, all in a curl.
Needing the toilet in the dark
She's in a fright and can't reach the light.
Then she dares to walk upstairs,
In her scary old house,
She decides to sneak,
As the door begins to creak.
On the wall she sees a shape
Just like a Dracula cape.
All of a sudden she feels a cold chill,
And she says, 'The vampire is going to kill me - it will.'
Wait . . . she hears her mum and the lights are on
And now she can go to the toilet,
All in the count of one.

Beth Hammett (11)
The Dale Primary School

MY BROTHER

My annoying brother Sean
He plays mowing the lawn,
His life is the PlayStation.
He plays Lego Creation,
His bedtime is eight o'clock
When I go upstairs, I give him a shock
He is six years old
And doesn't do what he's told.
My annoying brother Sean.

Callum Rogan (11)
The Dale Primary School

FEARS

See black figures in the night,
Faces in the curtains.
When you wake up in the night -
Do you get that feeling?
Do you hear the *tap, tap, tap*
Coming from downstairs?
Is it a burglar?
Is it a ghost?
Jump under the covers and wait until it's gone.

Paul Harrison (10)
The Dale Primary School

THE FANTASY

In the land of the clingfilm belly,
The kids stay up late to watch telly.
They eat steaks, they drink milk,
The pet snakes, they wear silk.
Their skin is so thin
They all cave in,
And they all drive around in a jelly!

Holly Sunderland (11)
The Dale Primary School

CHEMISTRY

It's time for chemistry once again
We're trying to blow up the lab.
Our teacher likes the sound of things
When they start to explode -
So he's the only one who stayed!

He claims to have brought back the dead
And Frankenstein's monster too,
So I'm glad for chemistry lessons
We're trying to blow up the lab.

Matthew Jones (11)
The Dale Primary School

LUNCH TIME

I love chocolate sundaes with Maltesers and a flake.
I love the taste of yummy fudge cake,
Delicious burgers with cheese and chips.
Which feel great when they touch your lips,
Yummy chocolate which melts in your mouth.
Deep fried fish from down south,
But then there's vegetables, especially sprouts
When I don't eat them, my mum always shouts.
They are disgusting, revolting
I think I'm gonna be sick!

Laura Bennett (10)
The Dale Primary School

MY DOG IS CALLED GEO

My dog is called Geo,
His little paws and his big eyes,
no one could despise.
He's playful and cute,
He's everything you need when you're alone,
He wags his tail and has a glimmer
in his eyes.
My best friend Geo.

Matthew Griffiths (10)
The Dale Primary School

SPIDERS

Creeping . . .
Planning to ambush you in your sleep.
Deadly . . .
Can't be seen.
Eight evil eyes which kill the first person
they set their gaze on.
Sssh! . . . They're coming!
Scuttling up your leg.
Getting ready to *bite!*
Fangs . . .
Inside a drooling mouth.
Clicking pincers,
Communicating without knowing.
Sssh! . . . They're coming!
What is the fear?
What is the scare?
Spiders.

Claire Faram (10)
The Dale Primary School

SEASONS

Summertime is here
Hot weather's near,
Holidays in sunny places
Lots of beach and water races.

Autumn leaves fall to the ground,
When you walk, a rustling sound.
Woolly hats and gloves are out,
Not many people are about.

Christmas snow and winter ice,
Not all of winter's nice.
Christmas trees and presents too
One for me and one for you.

Spring lambs are being born
Farmers are sowing their corn,
Sun is coming out
Rivers, may have a drought.

Sarah Bowler (10)
The Dale Primary School

THE TEDDY BEAR

You'd think if you were a teddy bear,
Your life would be easy, with no care.
But listen as I tell you of the story,
Of a bear, whose name was Roary.
'It's toy day!' his owner did say.
All the toys at Roary, did stare,
They didn't like the little teddy bear.
'She always takes you,' Barbie said,
Her face was turning a worrying red,
So the girl took Roary into the class, but hurried in,
A little too fast.
Out of the bag, Roary did fall, and he lay there -
In the hall.
But then a boy came by and picked him up
And in the *lost and found* he was put.
Then the little girl came
And shouted loudly, the bear's name
Roary!

Isabelle Willacy (10)
The Dale Primary School

HAMSTER ESCAPE

Tonight . . .
I plan to escape -
as I always do
There's so much more to explore out there
than being in this zoo.
Freedom . . .
It's a hole
I could squeeze through that
I'm on the edge, I'm flying
'Ouch!' I'm on the mat.
Paradise . . .
What's that I smell?
Is it cake or bread?
I'll fill my pouches 'til they're full
Tonight I'll be well fed.
Tired . . .
I need my bed
I'll scuttle back
Now the climb, a bookcase mountain.

These claws keep me on track
Exhausted . . .
I'm at the top
I'll sneak back in my nest
My secret's safe, I'll cover up my hole
Now I've earned my rest.

Rebecca Everett (11)
The Dale Primary School

I Think I'll Join The Army

'Gran, I think I'll join the army.'

'I don't think so, you're too barmy!
Anyway, the risks are too high
Because you may die!
Look at Uncle John, praying for aid
Didn't help him with his grenade.'

'But Gran!'

'Look at Grandad Spock
The time-bomb layer, he couldn't read clocks.'

'But Gran!'

'Look at Uncle Mack
Never knew his front from his back!'

'But Gran!'

'Look at Grandpa Wight,
The tank driver never knew his left from his right.'

'But Gran!'

'Yes love?'

'I only want a look
At being a cook!'

Mark Robinson (10)
The Dale Primary School

First Time Golfer

I get to the tee
I need a wee

But I pick up my club
And fall in a shrub

I take my shot
And land in a bunker

I play with the sand
And hurt my hand

I hit the ball
Then I hear a call

Then I hear a shout
And get knocked out.

Warren Parr (11)
The Dale Primary School

Cats
(Based on 'Cats Sleep Anywhere' by Eleanor Farjeon)

Cats sleep anywhere
Any table, any chair
On the carpet on the stairs
Any bush, any hedge
In your lap on the window ledge
Any cupboard, any drawer
On a rug or on the floor
Cats will sleep here
Cats will sleep here
Cats will sleep, anywhere.

Matthew Woolfenden (11)
The Dale Primary School

MONKEY

M oody as a mouse
O ut and about
N ibbling on a banana tree
K icking me
E verywhere they can't despair
Y our banana tree.

Joshua Adamson (9)
Weaverham Forest Primary School

THE POET'S GARDEN

The garden is looking particularly beautiful
at this time of the year. There are stained,
yellow blotches, as yellow as the sun. There
are red foxgloves in waving patterns. The lawn
is as green as a snooker table, with delicate,
studded yellow and white petals,
which gleam in the sun!

Abigail Edwards & Carolyn Tilston (10)
Weaverham Forest Primary School

A SUNSET

As colourful as the flaming fire
Beautiful like a newborn baby
Its rays as dazzling as the shining stars
As relaxing as a hot bath
As calm as the sea on a sunny day
Blending like the colours of a rainbow.

Jordan Furness (9)
Weaverham Forest Primary School

THINGS THAT GO BUMP IN THE NIGHT

I see ghosts float around my room,
touching all my stuff.
A swish of my curtain, a move of my shelf,
everything's shivering, even myself!
But I'm not afraid of the dark, not me!

Oh no! I think I feel something crawling
up at me.
But I'm not afraid of the dark, not me!

But now I've realised I'm not scared
of the night.
And ghouls and ghosts and nightmare monsters
run away in fright!
But I'm not afraid of the dark, not me!

Emily Mitchell (8)
Weaverham Forest Primary School

WHAT AM I

Mane as orange as the sun
Teeth like sharpened swords
Nose as black as a boot button
Eyes like a shiny, black stone
Fur like birds' feathers
Voice as frightening as an angry moose call
Tail like a furry hosepipe
Paws like a cat, but only bigger -
What am I?

Hannah Louise Rigby (9)
Weaverham Forest Primary School

MY SISTER

She's as nutty as a peanut
With eyes as sweet as sugar.
Cheeks as red as tomatoes
And hair like melted butter.
Her lips are like two, red buttons
as red as red can be.
Her teeth are sparkling white as
you can clearly see.

So now you know my sister
if you see her in the street.
Go up to her and make friends
because she's the person you'll
want to meet.

Sarah Baron (10)
Weaverham Forest Primary School

WHAT AM I?

Mane like a golden fireball
Eyes like piercing black beads
Nose as shiny as a boot button
Teeth like clashing blades
Fur as soft as birds' feathers
Mouth as frightening as a wicked grin
Body like a huge, cuddly toy
Paws like *big*, padded cushions
Claws like sharpened arrows
Tail like a *long, thick,* wiggly worm.

What am I?

Sarah Morris (9)
Weaverham Forest Primary School

MY FRIEND

S mile as bright as the sun
I ntelligent as a talking laptop
A rtistic as a child's toy
N egotiable as the queen

A ttractive as Marilyn Monroe
N eighbourly
D aring as stuntmen

C lever as a cat
H ome loving as a cuddly hamster
A crobatic like a circus queen
R apid and fast
L oving and caring.

Siân White & Charlotte Dunne (10)
Weaverham Forest Primary School